Values

A Programme for Primary Schools

Peter M. Clutterbuck

...lishing Limited
www.crownhouse.co.uk
www.chpus.com

First published by Blake Education in 2007 as
Values Book 1 (ISBN 978-174164158) and Values Book 2 (ISBN 978-141641586)

Current edition published 2008 by
Crown House Publishing Ltd
Crown Buildings, Bancyfelin, Carmarthen, Wales, SA33 5ND, UK
www.crownhouse.co.uk

British Library of Cataloguing-in-Publication Data
A catalogue entry for this book is available
from the British Library.

13-digit ISBN 978-184590082-3
10-digit ISBN 184590082-0

This edition is for sale in the United Kingdom and European Union only

Printed and bound in Great Britain by Cromwell Press, Trowbridge, Wiltshire

Contents

Contents

Section 2 SPECIFIC VALUES ACTIVITIES

About *this book*

A message to teachers

This is meant to be a practical book – a valuable resource full of ideas and activities to enhance the creation of learning environments that are caring, open, supportive and growth promoting.

It is important that all students are made aware of, and familiarised with, the many positive traits we refer to as **values**.

Being fully aware of the many values people hold in great esteem helps to make students selfless, tolerant and more caring human beings. Aspiring to certain values creates a healthy framework around which students can develop their daily interaction with both peers and adults.

A message to students

What are values?

Values are those behavioural traits, attitudes and concepts that have created the type of person you are. Your character is perceived in the minds of others by the presence or absence of these values within you. Are you caring, honest and reliable, possessing the numerous values that complement each other? Or are you perceived as someone unkind and not to be trusted?

Some of our innate values will be stronger and more obvious than others. A person who is scrupulously honest may not have the same strengths in assertiveness or tolerance.

Sometimes it takes a great deal of concentration and hard work to develop internal behaviours that will produce positive concepts of you in the minds of others. If someone conducted a survey of how other people rate the values you possess, which ones do you think would be rated more highly than others? Would your **honesty** be rated above or below such values as **courtesy**, **courage** or **assertiveness**?

Your successes in life will be influenced by the beliefs and attitudes you have about yourself and also the concepts others have of you. Therefore when you are completing activities in this book, think carefully about the things you can improve.

Values Education

SECTION 1

IDENTIFYING VALUES

This section includes activities designed to acquaint students with the concept of values behaviour in everyday interaction with others.

Lower primary

Upper primary or for more able students

Developing *personal values*

The following pages contain some ideas to help students understand and be aware of the importance of personal values when interacting with classmates and others. Although not labelled to specific values and traits, they are designed to develop in all students a caring, kind and open approach to others.

A *sensory awareness activity*

■ Meeting others

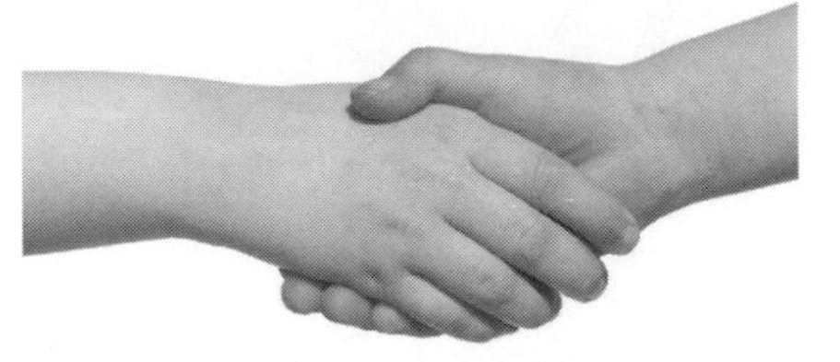

The entire class begins to walk around. Each person shakes both hands of a classmate they meet. They then shake the elbows of each person they meet, then their shoulders.

This is a great activity for the beginning of the year when classmates are still getting to know each other.

■ Touching

Have each pupil stand up and close their eyes. Ask them to touch something smooth, cold, rough, warm etc.

■ Trust walk

Have students pair off. One person is blindfolded. The other person takes their partner's hand and leads them on a walk around the school yard. The person leading must ensure their partner does not trip or fall. After 10 minutes the students swap places.

Identity *activities*

These activities help students answer the question *Who am I?*

Twenty Questions

Create 20 sentence starters that you want students to complete. Write them on the whiteboard or distribute photocopies.
Include topics such as:

a Things I really like:

I really like it when ____________________

My favourite day of the week is ____________________

I think it's really great when ____________________

b Things I hate:

I don't like it when ____________________

The food I hate most is ____________________

I get really upset when ____________________

c ***Me*** sentence starters:

The best thing about me is ____________________

The worst thing about me is ____________________

I am always ____________________

I do well in ____________________

I am proud that I am ____________________

I would really like to be able to ____________________

These types of questions, if handled properly, offer an opportunity for students to freely express themselves. They also provide teachers with an insight into each child's aspirations, qualities and values.

Family Tree

Provide students with a photocopy of a Family Tree structure. Explain to them what a family tree is. As a homework activity, the students ask their parents for the necessary information to complete their family tree.

Friendship *activities*

A strong knowledge of the qualities and values that create lasting friendships is most important for students to build healthy relationships with others.

Friendship books

Provide each pupil with a blank A4 piece of paper. In the top right-hand corner they write their name in very small letters – just large enough to be read.

Students hand their sheets back. These are jumbled and redistributed so each pupil receives someone else's sheet.

Each person must write three positive things about the pupil whose name is at the top of the page.

e.g. Joe always plays fair in games.
Joe is very strong.
Joe likes to help others.

Students then illustrate or decorate the page in some way. The pages are collected and kept by the teacher. After this activity has been done a number of times distribute the specific sheets back to each pupil. Have them do a front cover called MY FRIENDSHIP BOOK and staple all the sheets together to make a book they can keep. They can read the positive things said about them by others.

Friendship qualities

Students discuss what makes a friend. They write sentences that have starters such as:

a The things that make me such a good friend are:

____

b My best friend ____________________ is a good friend because he/she:

____

c I really like friends who:

____

d I could never be friends with someone who:

____

What are values?

Values are those qualities and traits that help make you a better person. They include such important things as honesty, friendliness, trustworthiness, courage and many more.

Imagine you are leaving your school to live overseas. You know you will most likely never see your friends again. How would you like your classmates to remember you?

In each box below is a message of farewell from one of your classmates. Choose the words from the Word Bank that you would like them to have written.

To my friend ___________, a most ___________ person. From Joseph
Goodbye. I will always remember you as a _________ person. From Sulla
Farewell to the most ____________ person I ever knew. From Carol
Good luck to _________, the most _________ person I know. From Ben
I'll be thinking of you. You are always so ___________. From Zachary
Have a great time. Thank you for your ___________. From Robyn

Word Bank

greedy friendship helpful courageous
kind honest generous nasty
forgiving trustworthy caring reliable

Values: A Programme for Primary Schools ISBN 978-184590082-3

Circle values

This activity will make you feel good about yourself and give you confidence. Ask an adult or classmate to fill in each circle.

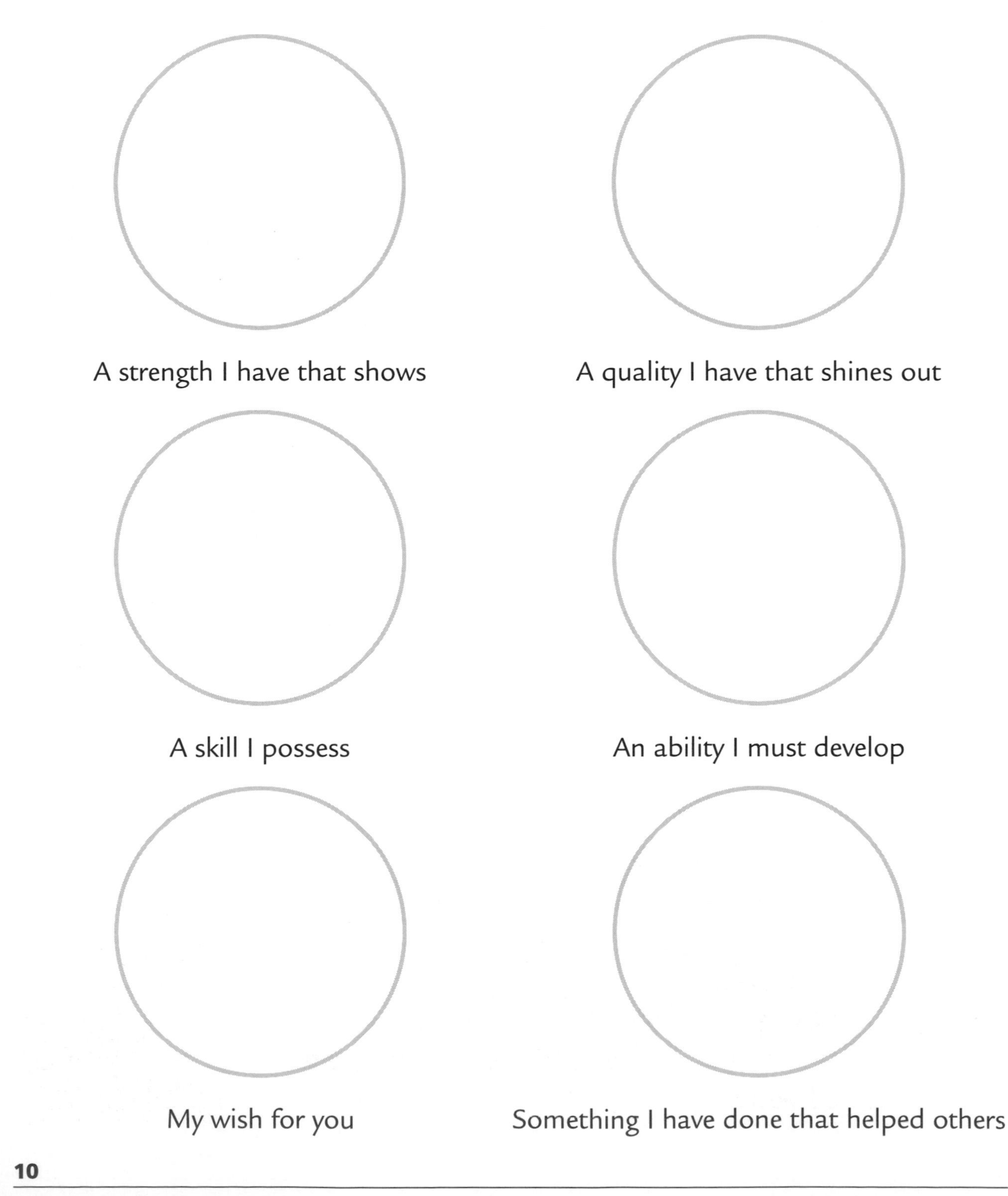

Values: A Programme for Primary Schools ISBN 978-1845900823

Valuing my possessions

Values: A Programme for Primary Schools ISBN 978-1845900823 © 2008 Blake Education and Crown House Publishing

Values jigsaw

In the map is a list of *values* words. Look at them carefully. Cut the map up and jumble the pieces. Challenge a classmate to arrange them correctly.

Do the right thing

You often hear people say, “Do the right thing!”

1 What does this mean? ______________________________

____

2 What are some values associated with it? Give examples.

____

____

____

3 Draw two pictures showing people doing the right thing.

A small-words activity

In the box are some small words that have been left out of the larger value words below. Add the small words in the correct spaces.

Word Bank					
one	air	pass	rust	eat	on
in	fast	age	path	as	our

1 The value that tells how we should meet danger without fear is cour_________.

2 A value that demands truthfulness and openness is h_________sty.

3 Politeness and good manners are a sign of c_________tesy.

4 Being able to account for your actions is resp_________sibilty.

5 A feeling of sorrow or pity for another facing difficulties is com_________ion.

6 Concern and thoughtfulness towards others is car_________g.

7 The ability to produce original learning is cr_________ivity.

8 A strong feeling of eager interest and effort is enthusi_________m.

9 Being completely free from bias, dishonesty or injustice is f_________ness.

10 The value of being firm in purpose, faith and loyalty is stead_________ness.

11 The value of being able to understand how another is feeling is called sym_________y.

12 When at all times you are reliable, you show others how t_________worthy you are.

Values: A Programme for Primary Schools ISBN 978-184590082-3

Me and my values

In each group colour the block next to the words that describe you.
Be honest when you answer.

1
- ☐ always reliable
- ☐ sometimes reliable
- ☐ not reliable

2
- ☐ always truthful
- ☐ sometimes truthful
- ☐ not truthful

3
- ☐ always friendly to others
- ☐ sometimes friendly to others
- ☐ never friendly to others

4
- ☐ a hard worker
- ☐ an average worker
- ☐ a poor worker

5
- ☐ always polite and courteous to others
- ☐ usually polite and courteous to others
- ☐ rarely polite to others

6
- ☐ good self-control
- ☐ fair self-control
- ☐ poor self-control

7
- ☐ always helpful to others
- ☐ sometimes helpful to others
- ☐ rarely helpful to others

8
- ☐ always willing to listen to others
- ☐ usually listens to others
- ☐ never listens to others

9
- ☐ always clean and tidy
- ☐ usually clean and tidy
- ☐ often clean and tidy

10
- ☐ enthusiastic towards all things at school
- ☐ enthusiastic to some things at school
- ☐ don't like doing anything at school

Occupational values

What values do you expect the following people to have? Colour the one you think is most important. Give a brief reason for your choice.

1 a teacher — generosity fairness flexibility

____

2 a doctor — honesty thankfulness helpfulness

____

3 a parent — understanding courtesy excellence

____

4 a train driver — kindness reliability patience

____

5 a football coach — enthusiasm orderliness honesty

____

6 a policeman — honesty creativity cleanliness

____

7 tuckshop manager — self-discipline courtesy cleanliness

____

8 a team member — thankfulness determination generosity

____

9 a pilot — courtesy tact responsibility

____

10 a postman — honesty punctuality kindness

____

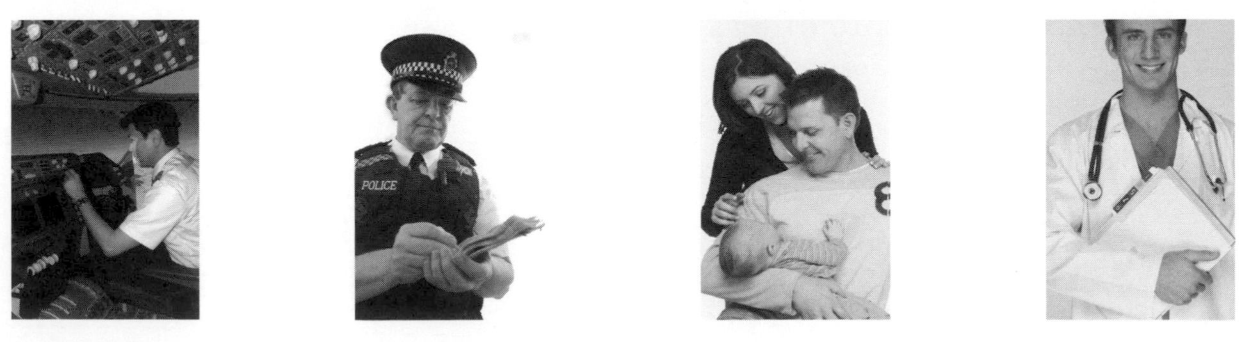

Animal values

Look at each picture. Can the animal or object pictured possess values? Tick **Yes** or **No** and then explain why.

1 Can a dog be loyal?

☐ Yes ☐ No
Why? ____________________
____

2 Can a cat be helpful?

☐ Yes ☐ No
Why? ____________________
____

3 Can a car be reliable?

☐ Yes ☐ No
Why? ____________________
____

4 Can an eagle be caring?

☐ Yes ☐ No
Why? ____________________
____

5 Can a horse be determined?

☐ Yes ☐ No
Why? ____________________
____

6 Can a monkey be friendly?

☐ Yes ☐ No
Why? ____________________
____

Values: A Programme for Primary Schools ISBN 978-184590082-3

Which value is needed?

Look closely at the values in the box. Decide which values you would expect a friend to have if you asked him or her to do the following. Answer on the back of this sheet.

Word Bank

forgiveness	punctuality	thankfulness	patience
trustworthiness	sympathy	responsibility	enthusiasm

Begin: I would expect my friend...

1 You are learning to skip. Your friend is helping you but you are not very good at it.

2 Your friend forgot to bring his lunch on the school trip. You happily let him eat half of yours.

3 Your family is going to the football tomorrow. Your friend has asked if she can come. You agree but she must be at your place no later than ten a.m.

4 You ask a friend to look after your baby brother for ten minutes while you help your mother get some things from the car.

5 You have asked your friend to be in your Saturday morning "gang" in which you do lots of fun things.

6 A car has run over and killed your puppy. You are very upset.

7 Your friend lent you his cricket bat. When you were playing with it you accidentally chipped it when you missed the ball and hit the wicket.

8 You have allowed your friend to take home your new expensive laser pen. You have asked her to be very careful with it, not to let anyone else use it and to bring it back tomorrow.

Make it personal

1 Answer these questions honestly about yourself.

a Are you friendly? _______

b Are you fair in games? _______

c Are you kind to others? _______

d Are you honest in games and schoolwork? _______

e Are you loyal to others? _______

f Do you tell the truth? _______

g Do you help out even when you don't want to? _______

2 Write the initials of a person you know whom you think has each quality.

determined	courteous	thoughtful	caring

3 Write a paragraph titled *The Perfect Person*. Describe a person who has all the values listed above.

____

____

____

____

____

____

Values: A Programme for Primary Schools ISBN 978-1845900823

Placing my values in order

Depending on who we are, we may consider some values more important than others. For example, a teacher may think **honesty** is your most valuable trait, while a sports coach may consider your **perseverance** the most important value you possess.

Read the ten values written in the box. Write them from 1 to 10 in order of importance to you (1 being the most important and 10 being the least important).

List them again in the order you think your parents would choose for you, then once more in the order you think your friends would choose.

Word Bank

honesty enthusiasm cleanliness forgiveness confidence
courtesy truthfulness reliability friendliness patience

	The values I have that are important to me.	The values I have that are important to my parents.	The values I have that are important to my friends.
1			
2			
3			
4			
5			
6			
7			
8			
9			
10			

Values: A Programme for Primary Schools ISBN 978-184590082-3

Opposites

Although some words name or describe positive values, others name or describe negative values.

Match each word on the left to its opposite on the right.

1	courageous	enemy
2	kind	hate
3	friend	give up
4	have a go	rude
5	enthusiastic	ungrateful
6	courteous	cowardly
7	thankful	unforgiving
8	forgiving	mediocre
9	honest	cruel
10	giving	disinterested
11	love	dishonest
12	excellent	selfish

Values: A Programme for Primary Schools ISBN 978-184590082-3

Our expectations of things

Things we use every day are expected to have certain qualities. For example, you would expect a chair to be **comfortable**.

Briefly describe the qualities we want the following things to have.

1 Car ______________________________________

____

2 Video game ______________________________________

____

3 Hamburger ______________________________________

____

4 Newspaper ______________________________________

____

5 Book ______________________________________

____

6 Classroom ______________________________________

____

7 Knife ______________________________________

____

8 Bicycle ______________________________________

____

9 Pear ______________________________________

____

10 Bed ______________________________________

____

Displaying values 1

Read each passage carefully. Decide what value you think each person has displayed. The words in the box at the bottom of the page will help. Write your answers in sentences. Say what kind of person each is.

1 Jihan found money in the playground. She immediately took it to the staffroom and gave it to her teacher.

____

2 The teacher left the room. Some of the students began to talk loudly and run around. Miffy made them sit down and get on with their work.

____

3 Francisco was carrying a large box of books that he was told to take back to the school library. Without being asked, Sally opened the door for him.

____

4 Jake broke Cynthia's new ruler. When he apologised, Cynthia said, "Don't worry, I know you didn't mean to break it".

____

5 A new pupil started in the class. Rhianna asked her to come and play with all the others at lunch time.

____

6 Although the teenagers were much bigger and older than him, Robert stopped them from hurting the injured bird.

____

Word Bank

forgiveness	friendliness	helpfulness
courage	responsibility	honesty

7 Write a passage like the one above to describe the value courtesy.

____

____

____

____

Values: A Programme for Primary Schools ISBN 978-184590082-3 © 2008 Blake Education and Crown House Publishing

Displaying values 2

Read each passage. Decide what value you feel each person has displayed. The words in the box at the bottom of the page will help. Write your answers in a sentence.

1 On his way home from school, Mike found an abandoned kitten. He took it home and fed it. Later he took it to the RSPCA.

___

2 Although her younger brother was taking a long time to do up his shoes, Claudia was quite happy to wait for him.

___

3 When he refereed the football match, the teacher did not favour either team even though one team consisted of boys from his class.

___

4 When George saw the supply teacher arrive in the car park, he went over and helped her carry a large box of books. He showed her where the classroom was.

___

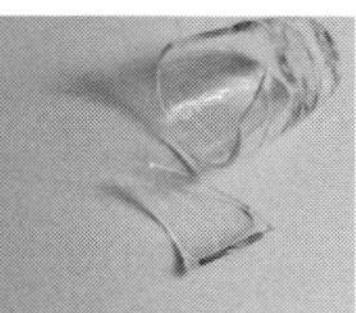

5 When the teacher asked who had dropped the glass and broken it, while she was out of the room, Jeremy immediately owned up.

___

6 On Saturdays for the last six months, Billy has worked as a delivery person for the local chemist. In that time he has never missed a day's work, and he has never been late.

___

Word Bank		
truthfulness	courtesy	caring
reliability	patience	fairness

7 Write a passage like the ones above to describe the value **determination**.

___

___

Values: A Programme for Primary Schools ISBN 978-184590082-3

A values poem

Values can be expressed through poetry.

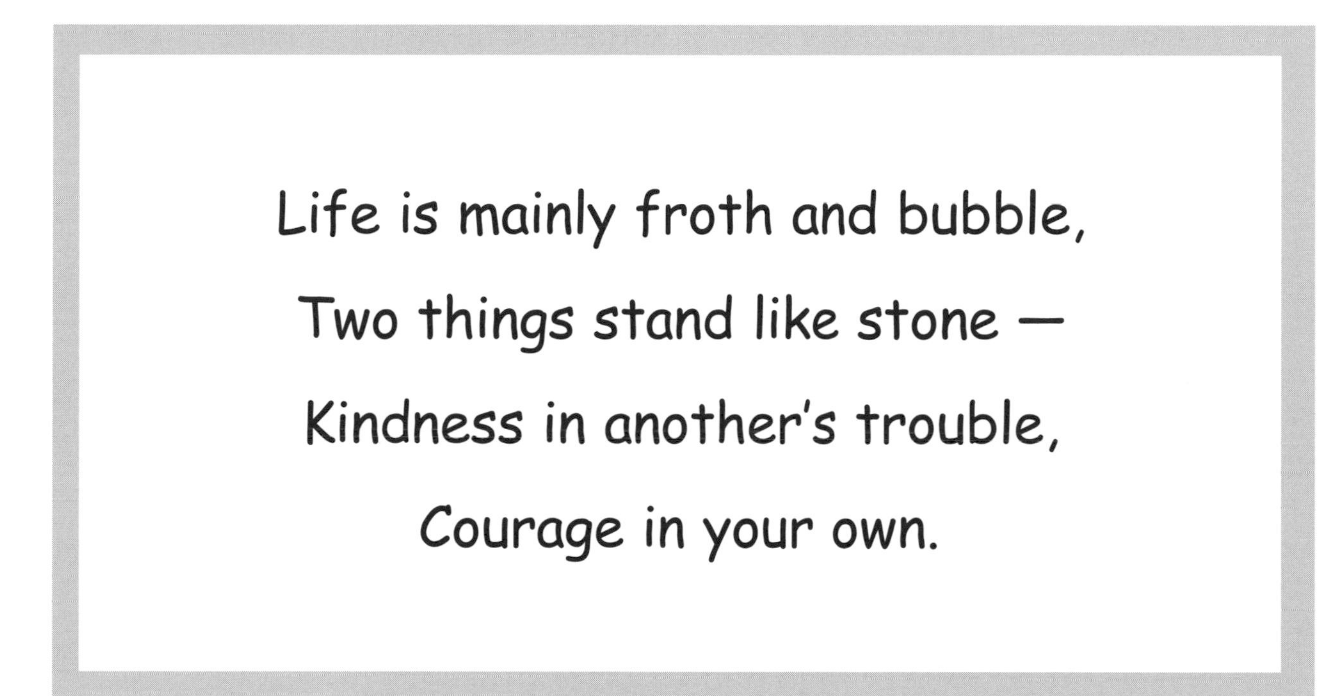

1 Have you ever helped someone who was troubled? Describe what the problems were and what you did.

____

____

____

2 Have you ever had to face troubles of your own? Describe what they were and what you did.

____

____

____

3 Write the above saying in large coloured letters on a sheet of paper. Surround it with a colourful border. Display your poster in the classroom.

My life story

An autobiography is a good way of telling people about yourself, so they have a better understanding of you. Here is a questionnaire for you to answer.

1 My name ______________________________

and my birth date ______________________________

2 I am ____________ years old.

3 Five words that best describe me are ______________________________

____

4 I spend my time after school and on weekends by ______________________________

____

5 My best friend is ______________________________

____

6 Something all my friends have in common is ______________________________

____

7 The magazines or books that I like reading regularly are ______________________________

____

8 My favourite sports, games and hobbies are ______________________________

____

9 My main aim over the next six months is to achieve ______________________________

____

10 My most important aim for my future is ______________________________

____

11 The thing about me that makes people like me is ______________________________

____

12 The thing that people don't like about me is ______________________________

____

My family tree

It is important to value family relationships. One way of doing this is to complete a family tree. Your parents and extended family will help you complete this family tree.

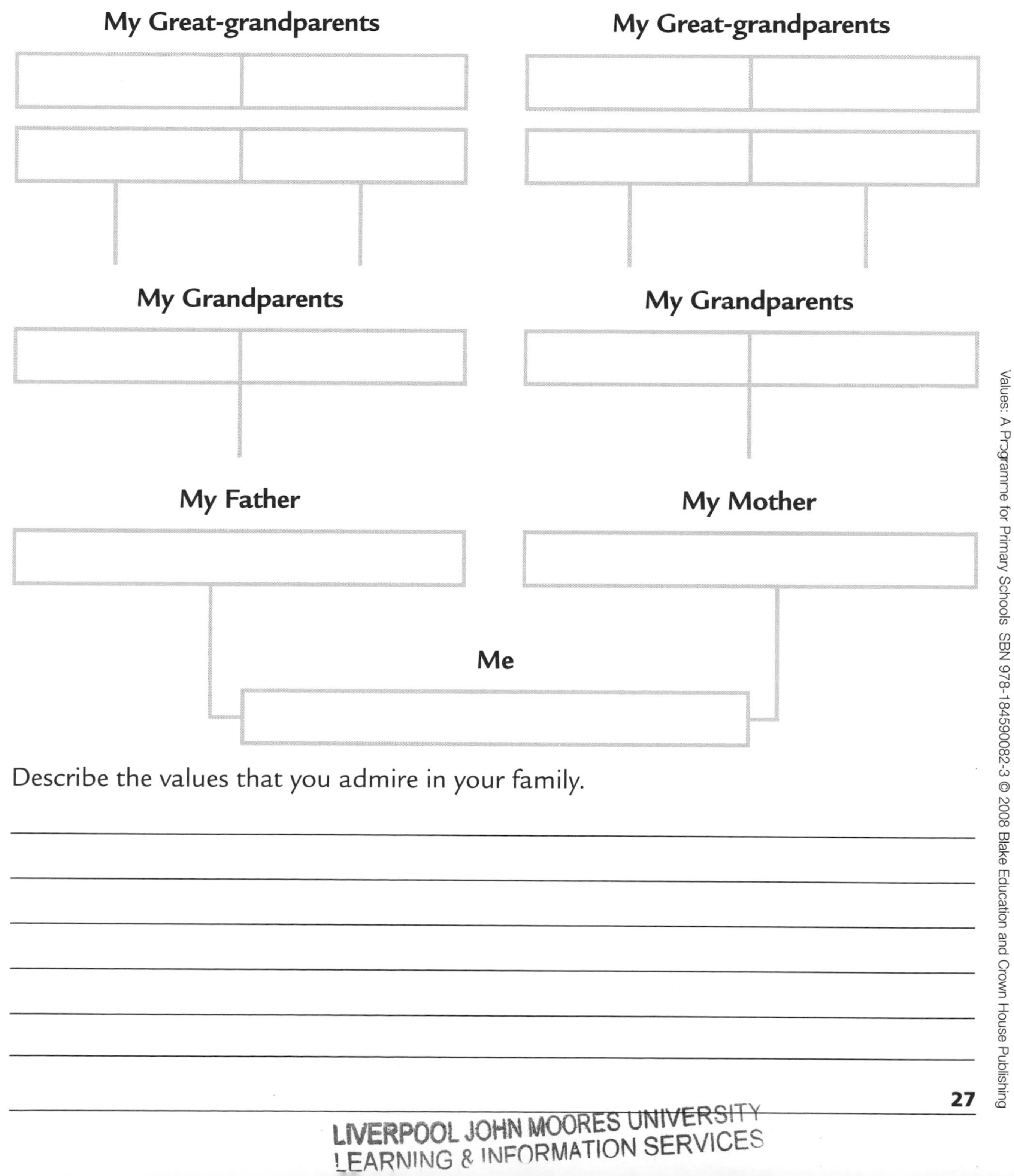

Describe the values that you admire in your family.

Values questionnaire

What are your values? Make sure you give honest answers to each of these questions.

1 You find money in the street. Would you:
- ☐ keep it
- ☐ spend it
- ☐ give it to an adult

2 You see someone carrying some large boxes and they trip over. Would you:
- ☐ laugh
- ☐ run to tell others how funny it was
- ☐ offer to help the person

3 You see your best friend being bullied by a group of big kids. Would you:
- ☐ move away quickly
- ☐ tell a teacher
- ☐ rush to help your friend

4 You see a classmate fall over in the playground. Would you:
- ☐ point at them and laugh
- ☐ tell them they are clumsy
- ☐ help them up and ask if they are OK

5 You see a classmate drawing on the toilet wall. Would you:
- ☐ not tell anyone
- ☐ tell a teacher
- ☐ tell your classmate to stop doing it

6 You borrowed a friend's video game and damaged it accidentally. Would you:
- ☐ keep it and say you'd lost it
- ☐ give it back and not say anything
- ☐ give it back and explain what happened

7 You are invited to a party but your best friend isn't. Would you:
- ☐ tell your friend
- ☐ not tell your friend
- ☐ ask the person having the party if your friend could come too

8 A classmate accidentally squirts some sauce on your new clothes. Would you:
- ☐ scream at them and tell them they are stupid
- ☐ never talk to them again
- ☐ say you know accidents can happen

9 You are playing an important football game tomorrow. Would you:
- ☐ tell others your side is sure to lose
- ☐ tell others you won't win
- ☐ tell others that you will be trying hard

10 Your mother makes you take your little brother with you to play with your friends. Would you:
- ☐ tell him to clear off or you'll hurt him
- ☐ offer him a chocolate to stay home
- ☐ invite him to join in the games

Values: A Programme for Primary Schools ISBN 978-184590082-3 © 2008 Blake Education and Crown House Publishing

Values test

These questions will help you decide the values that are most important to you. There are no right or wrong answers but you must be honest.

1 Your best friend has just left his orange skin and sandwich wrapper on the school playing field. What will you do?

2 A neighbour has had to go away suddenly and their letterbox is full of post. What will you do?

3 You find a wallet with money and some credit cards in it. What will you do with it?

4 Your friend is threatened by a bully. They ask you to help. What will you do?

5 You fooled about when the teacher left the room. When she came back she asked if you had kept working. What will you say?

6 Estaban, a new boy from Chile, wants to play football in your team. He doesn't know the rules and can't kick the ball properly. What will you do?

7 Your coach has taught you how to shoot a goal but you just don't get the hang of it. What will you do?

8 A good friend tells you they stole some magazines from the newsagent. They want you to swear not to tell. What will you do?

Expressing my values

Things may upset us because of the values we hold strongly.

If we watch a television programme and it shows people in another country starving or suffering, we may feel angry because governments are not doing more to help.

If you see a person treating a dog cruelly, it may also anger you because you value the relationships between humans and pets.

If you see a truck dumping rubbish into a stream, and if you value our environment, you would be extremely angry.

Complete each of the following sentences in your own words. Relate your answers to your values.

1 I get angry when ______________________________

____

2 It worries me that ______________________________

____

3 I don't like ______________________________

____

4 It really makes me angry when ______________________________

____

5 I am disappointed that ______________________________

____

6 I feel really strongly about ______________________________

____

7 When people don't agree with me ______________________________

____

8 I don't like people who ______________________________

____

Name

Date

Personal interview

Imagine you are a famous movie star being interviewed and you are asked the following questions. Write your answers on the lines.

Interviewer: What do you like about being a famous movie star?
Me: ______________________________

____

Interviewer: Are there any disadvantages in being so famous?
Me: ______________________________

____

Interviewer: Have you ever done anything to help people who are less fortunate than you are?
Me: ______________________________

____

Interviewer: What contribution have you made to the environment?
Me: ______________________________

____

Interviewer: What talents are important for you as a movie actor?
Me: ______________________________

____

Interviewer: What values do you consider are important to you when working with other actors?
Me: ______________________________

____

Interviewer: What characteristics do you value most in a friend?
Me: ______________________________

____

Values – personal interview

1 Which of these do you consider your strongest value?

honesty	reliability	thankfulness

Why?

____

____

2 Who has been the greatest influence on your life in helping to build the values you treasure?

____

Explain how this person helped you.

____

____

3 Which of these values do you consider least important?

responsibility	self-discipline	truthfulness

Why?

____

____

4 Which of the following values is most appreciated by your parents?

forgiveness	excellence	determination	respect

Why?

____

____

Values: A Programme for Primary Schools ISBN 978-184590082-3

Questions about values

Think carefully about values as you complete the questions on this page.

1 Can a homeless, poor person have any values? Explain.

2 What values can a dog, cat or any other animal have?

3 Could a terrorist have values? Explain.

4 Do you think young children have a stronger sense of values than teenagers? Explain.

5 Do you think young children have a stronger sense of values than adults? Explain.

6 Of the values you've learnt about, which one is the most important to you? Why?

7 What values do you think that people coming to another country need?

How to conduct an interview

An interview is a structured conversation between two people for the purpose of learning something. If you are an interviewer you must be careful about the questions you ask in order to get the information you want.

Consider these questions.

A. What is your name? Is netball the sport you like best?	**B.** Tell me a bit about yourself. Describe the sport you like best.

Set B questions would give you more information as they require more than a simple Yes or No response.

Activity

- Choose a member of your family to interview. Ask a minimum of eight questions. Your aim as the interviewer is to find out as much information as you can about this person's life.
- Make sure each of your questions requires more than a simple *Yes* or *No* answer.
- When you are conducting the interview you may find you need to add extra questions. e.g. If you are interviewing someone about arriving from another country you may want to ask further questions about their life in the country they came from.
- When you have completed your interview, write out your questions and answers. You may wish to keep a tape of the interview to check the information later in case you have forgotten to write something down.

Adult values challenge

Interview two adults. Find out what they value, where their values came from and how their values have changed.

PERSON A	PERSON B
Name	Name

What values do you consider most important in today's world?

What values do you think some young people lack?

How have your values changed since you left school?

Have your values changed in the last two years?

What do you think should be done to make young people more aware of values?

Values: A Programme for Primary Schools ISBN 978-184590082-3

Family member interview

Learn more about a person in your family. Explain to them that you are learning about values and ask them the following questions.

Person being interviewed:

____

1 What is something you do well?

____

2 What is something you would like to be able to do better?

____

3 Are you always honest and truthful?

____

4 Would you ever tell a lie to protect a friend?

____

5 Who has had the greatest influence on your life?

____

6 What values do you think a friend should possess?

____

7 What special quality in people do you value most of all?

____

8 What values do you think young people today should be taught?

____

9 In what ways were you taught values?

____

Thank you for your time.

Who?

We are taught about values by people close to us: parents, teachers, friends, a football coach and so on.

Who taught you about each value? In some cases there may be more than one person. When do you think you first learnt about this value?

Value	Who Taught Me	When
Honesty		
Courtesy		
Fairness		
Courage		
Friendliness		
Reliability		
Pride		
Patience		
Loyalty		
Responsibility		
Truthfulness		
Self-discipline		
Tolerance		

Write a paragraph describing a person whom you admire.
Say why you admire them and name the values they possess.

Where?

We can learn about values in many different places like at home, school, the playground, church and clubs.

Choose some of the values from the box and write them next to the place where you think you learnt about them.

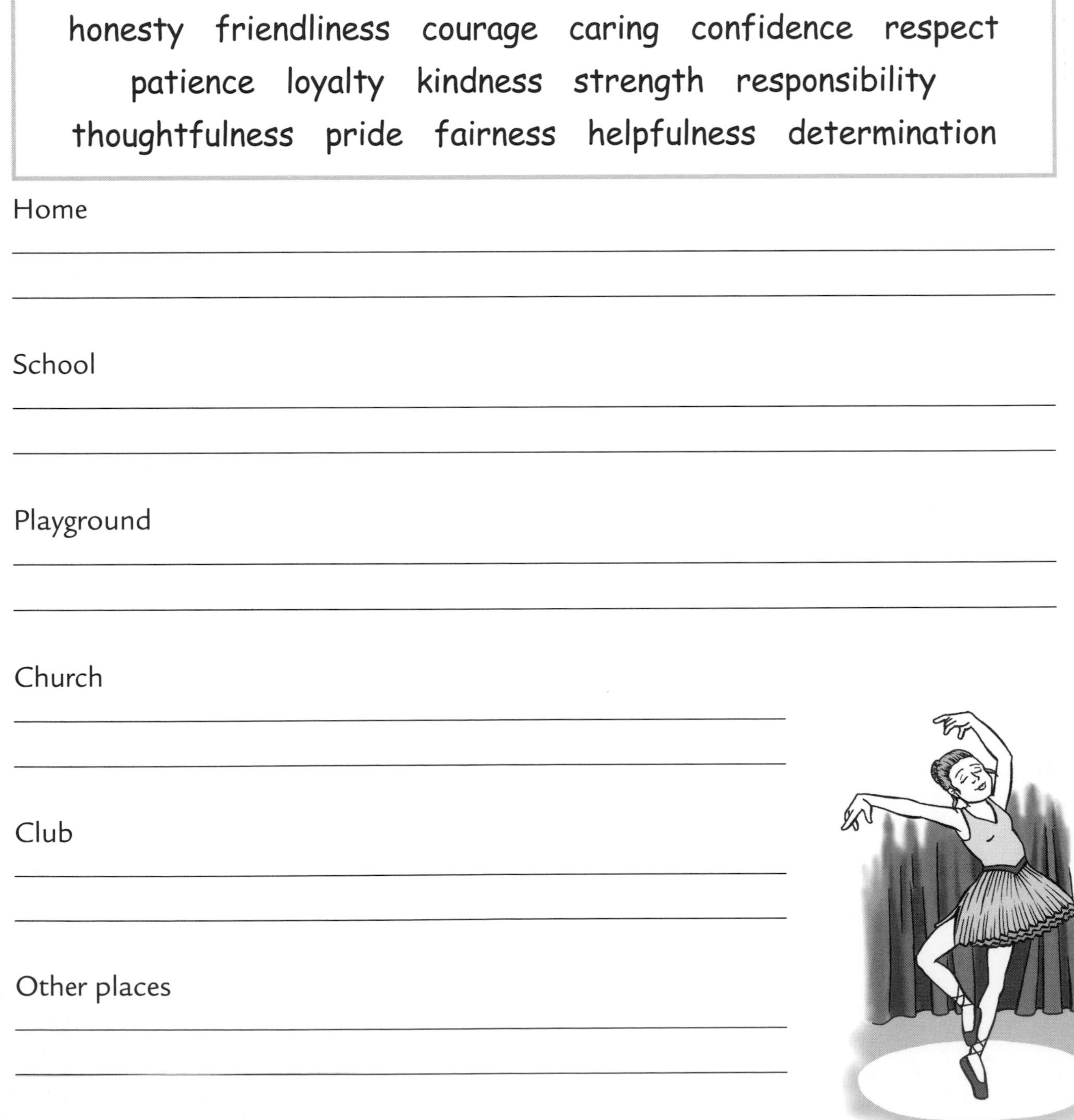

honesty friendliness courage caring confidence respect
patience loyalty kindness strength responsibility
thoughtfulness pride fairness helpfulness determination

Home

____

____

School

____

____

Playground

____

____

Church

____

____

Club

____

____

Other places

____

____

Values: A Programme for Primary Schools ISBN 978-184590082-3 © 2008 Blake Education and Crown House Publishing

What do these people value?

Certain behaviours and characteristics are clues to the things we value.

From the box choose what each person values.

animal rights equality health environment possessions success wealth freedom

1 Elisa always makes us clean up the playing field after lunch. On the weekend she helps local people plant trees to regenerate growth along a stream. Elisa values the ____________________

2 When Ryan was younger, he did a silly thing and was sent to prison for three years. When he got out he said, "I'm never ever going to do anything silly again. I don't want to go back to jail!" Ryan values his ____________________

3 Each day Gemma exercises before school. She makes sure she eats only healthy foods. Gemma values her ____________________

4 Deb has a bank account in which she puts her pocket money. She always does jobs to get extra money to put into the account. One day she hopes to be rich. Deb values ____________________

5 John is a member of the Junior RSPCA. He gets very upset when he hears that animals are treated badly. John values ____________________

6 Jacki treats all people with respect. She does a lot to help immigrants settle into their new country. She believes everyone should have the same opportunities. Jacki values ____________________

7 Bradley has big dreams for the future. His goals are to be wealthy and a famous film star. Bradley values ____________________

8 Bruno has a lot of swap cards which he keeps in a box. He also has lots of toys but he won't let anyone play with them. Bruno values ____________________

Changing values

Our lives change with time. The toy that was important to you five years ago is probably not important to you today. Some of the friends you had five years ago you may not even see today.

Do you think the values you possess now will change in any way? Tick a box then give a reason.

Likely to Change

Value	Yes	No	Why?
Honesty			
Respect			
Courage			
Loyalty			
Reliability			
Kindness			
Tolerance			
Fairness			

Values: A Programme for Primary Schools ISBN 978-184590082-3

Negative values

Sometimes we are thoughtless in the replies we give to other people. Even if you do not agree with someone or do what they ask, always be tactful and courteous.

Write what you would have said.

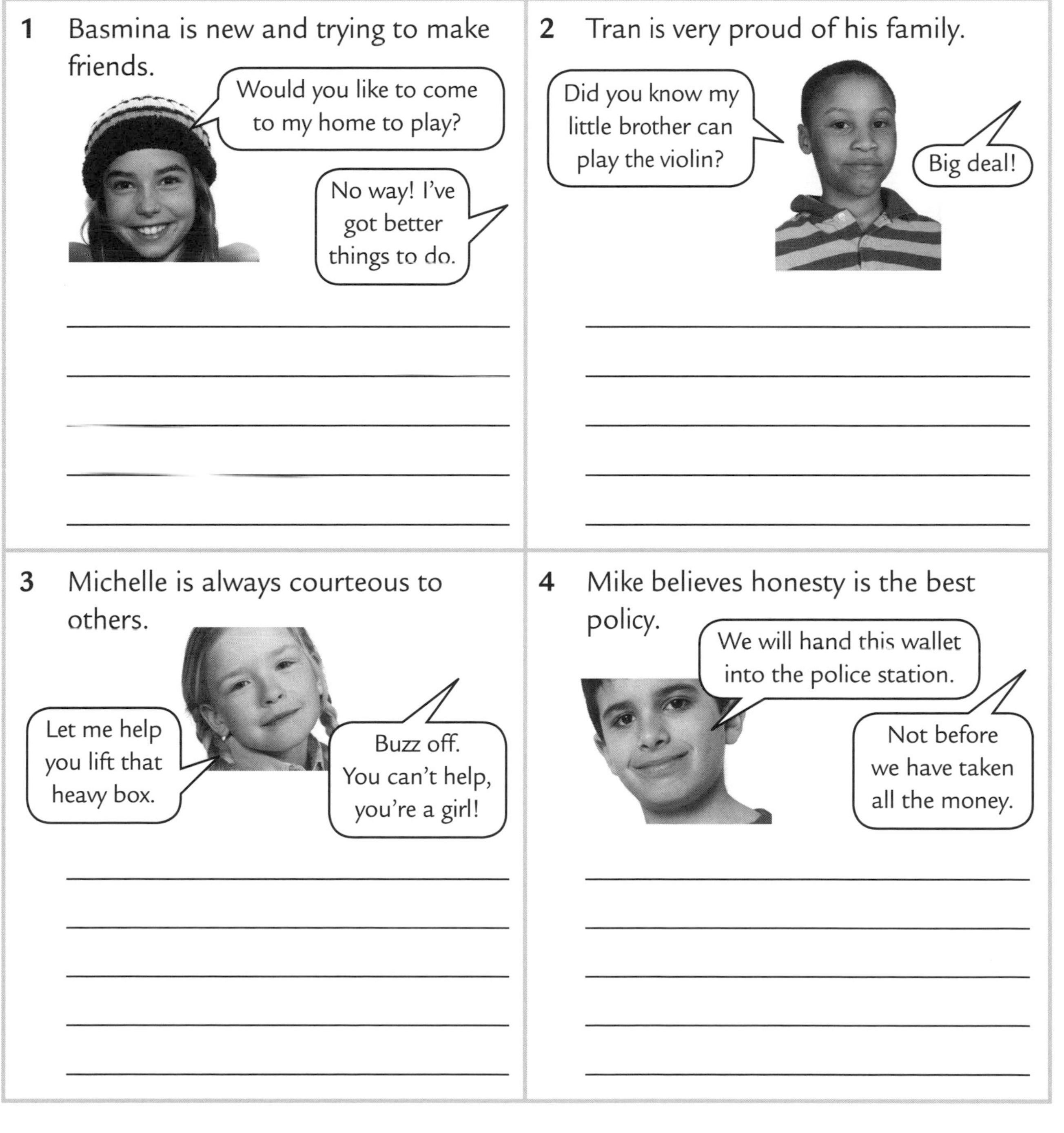

Values: A Programme for Primary Schools ISBN 978-184590082-3

Our national values

Do you value your country? What do you do to show that your country means a lot to you?

President John F Kennedy once told Americans,
"Ask not what your country can do for you; ask what you can do for your country."

1 What values do you think are important to our way of life and why?

____

____

____

2 Do you think all people in your country have the same values? Why?

____

____

____

3 What are some things you do, or have done, to show that you value your country and are proud to be from here?

____

____

____

4 Draw and colour your country's flag.

How to develop your own values

We should choose those values which best suit our way of life. These should include core values e.g. **honesty** **truthfulness** **kindness** **tolerance**.

People will know and respect us for the values we have.

- Be true to yourself and pay attention to your feelings. The way you feel about things will help you determine your values.
- Think about other people; especially those you like or admire. What is it about them that makes you like them? Can you be like them too?
- Listen to your parents. Discuss important issues in your life with them. Be open to their points of view just as you expect them to consider yours.
- If you are listening to the daily news or reading a newspaper focus on those things that interest you or upset you. This will help you decide what is important to you.
- Talk to others – your family, relatives, friends and classmates – about important issues. Listen to them and try to understand their points of view. Be open to criticism of your own views. They may only be trying to help you.
- Don't be afraid to express your opinions on issues that interest or upset you, but don't try to impose your opinions on others.

Remember: You can disagree without being disagreeable!

If you firmly believe in something, don't walk away from your beliefs just because others disagree or mock you.

Remember: Strength and truth always win out!

Share your ideas and enthusiasm with others.

Remember: The best way to forget about your own problems is to help someone else solve theirs.

Personal timelines

Completing a personal timeline can be an important preliminary activity to writing an autobiography.

You can work as a whole class or in small groups. Sit in a circle and begin by discussing the personal experiences that you have all had in your lives.

Choose people to describe their feelings when they first learnt to ride a bike; began school; played in a sporting team; made a good friend; received an award etc.

Encourage everyone who wants to talk to share experiences that involved their feelings.

Did these change your attitude to yourself or to other people?

When the discussion is over, record your own timeline on a large sheet of paper.

Begin on the left with your birth and record all the significant events up to today.

Display your timelines in the classroom.

Now you can make a **Class Group Timeline**.

Fasten a piece of string across one wall of your classroom. One end of the string is *birth* and the other is *today*. Use cards and paperclips to decorate the string with events that you all consider important from your past.

You might like to extend the string and add events that you think may occur in the *future*.

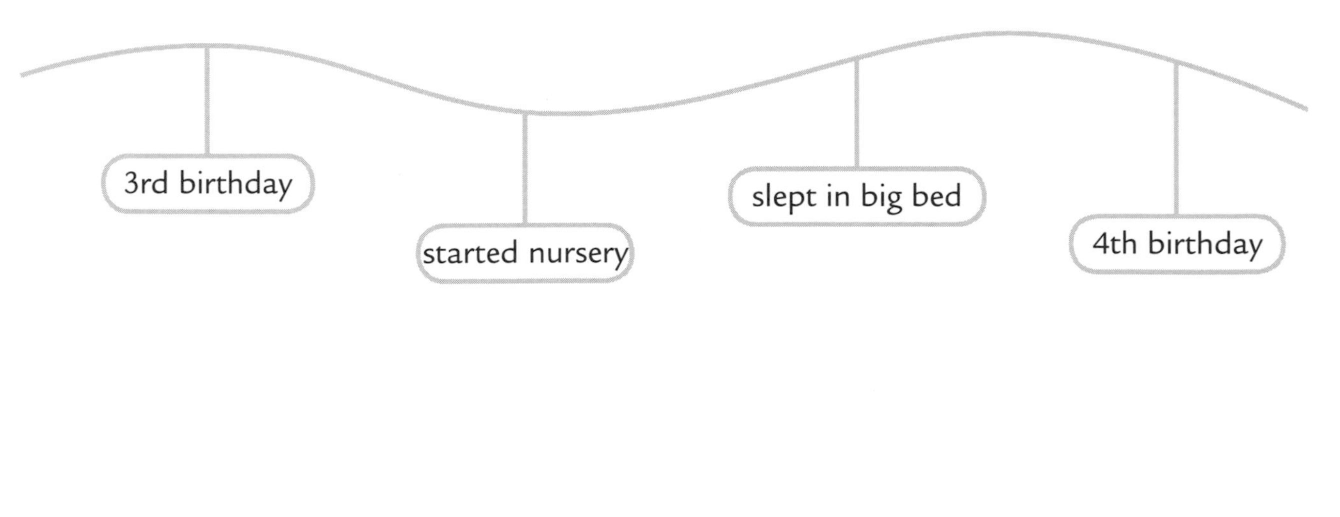

Positive and negative values

1 In the grid are positive values and negative values. Colour red those values you believe are positive ones. Colour grey those that are negative.

helpfulness	jealousy	caring	honesty
compassion	patience	kindness	fairness
courage	hypocrisy	reliability	deceit
respect	cowardice	cruelty	responsibility
boastfulness	tact	openness	hatred
self-discipline	arrogance	anger	determination
mistrust	enthusiasm	laziness	forgiveness
creativity	courtesy	perseverance	cleanliness

2 Find the word **moderation** in your dictionary and write its meaning.

____

3 How many words can you make by using the letters in **moderation**?

____

____

____

Determining values

What values should you possess in the following situations?
Use the values in this box to help you with your answers.

patience	courage	helpfulness	friendliness
trustworthiness	courtesy	forgiveness	determination

1 You are left alone at home one dark night. You hear a strange noise outside.

2 Your mother is not feeling well. There is a lot of work to be done around the house.

3 You are helping your young brother learn to ride a bicycle.

4 A boy, new to your school, tells you he feels lonely.

5 You are playing a game when another player accidentally hits your nose.

6 Your legs are aching but your athletics team needs you to try to win the race so they'll get more points.

7 You are sitting chatting to friends on a crowded bus. A lady who is pregnant is standing nearby as there are no seats left.

8 You are given the job of taking the school tuckshop money to the office.

Values: A Programme for Primary Schools ISBN 978-184590082-3

My checklist 1

How do you rate yourself as a values performer? Do you feel you are strong in certain areas but can improve in others? Are you always honest and courteous with others? How do you think your parents, teacher and best friends would rate you in each one?

To assess your values performance complete the following.

Performance rating (put a ✓ in the correct box)

	My Own Rating		**My Parents**		**My Teacher**		**My Friends**	
	Strong	Can Do Better	Strong	Can Do Better	Strong	Can Do Better	Strong	Can Do Better
assertive								
caring								
compassionate								
confident								
courageous								
courteous								
creative								
determined								
enthusiastic								
fair								
flexible								
forgiving								
friendly								
generous								
helpful								
honest								
kind								
independent								

My checklist 2

How do you rate yourself as a values performer? Do you always feel you are strong in certain areas but can improve in others? Are you always honest and courteous with others? How do you think your parents, teachers and best friends would rate you in each one?

To assess your values performance complete the following.

Performance rating (put a ✓ in the correct box)

	My Own Rating		**My Parents**		**My Teacher**		**My Friends**	
	Strong	Can Do Better	Strong	Can Do Better	Strong	Can Do Better	Strong	Can Do Better
loyal								
open								
patient								
persevering								
purposeful								
reliable								
responsible								
self-disciplined								
steadfast								
strong								
tactful								
thankful								
tolerant								
thoughtful								
trustworthy								
truthful								

Identifying values

In the box are some values we should aspire to.
Write each value beside its definition.

compassion caring fairness
courtesy patience creativity
enthusiasm forgiveness
courage thankfulness

1 ______________ calm endurance without complaint – calmness when waiting

2 ______________ an expression, through words or actions, of grateful feelings

3 ______________ to cease having bad feelings against someone else

4 ______________ a feeling of sorrow or pity for another who is facing difficulty

5 ______________ concern and thoughtfulness towards everyone

6 ______________ the ability to meet danger and difficulty without fear

7 ______________ politeness and good manners when dealing with other people

8 ______________ a strong feeling of interest and effort for something

9 ______________ to be completely free from dishonesty or injustice

10 ______________ the ability to produce something original

Questioning *your values*

These four pages contain a list of values.
Would other people think you have these qualities?
Think carefully about each one.

Assertiveness
Do you stand up for things you believe in?

Caring
Do you care when others are unhappy or need help?

Compassion
Are you sad when you know others who are having a bad time?

Confidence
Are you sure of yourself and what you can do?

Consideration
Do you think about how other people will react to your words or actions?

Courage
Are you brave even when things frighten you?

Courtesy
Are you polite and well-mannered?

Creativity
Do you follow your own ideas and not copy others?

Determination
Do you keep going even when things get tough?

Enthusiasm
Are you eager and happy to do things?

Questioning *your values* *cont*

Excellence

Do you want everything you do to be your best?

Fairness

Are you able to see both sides of a situation or argument?

Flexibility

Can you change if you see a better way?

Forgiveness

If someone has done you wrong, can you accept an apology?

Friendliness

Are you happy to meet and become friendly with new people?

Generosity

Can you be unselfish and share with others?

Helpfulness

Are you willing to help even when it is something you don't like doing?

Honesty

Do you always do the right thing?

Kindness

Are you gentle and big-hearted?

Loyalty
Do you keep your promises and stand by your friends?

Open-mindedness
Are you willing to listen to new ideas?

Patience
Can you wait for things calmly?

Perseverance
Do you continue with a difficult task until it is finished?

Peacefulness
Can you become calm and friendly after having a quarrel?

Purposefulness
Can you keep going in order to get the right result?

Pride
Do you feel good about your achievements?

Reliability
Can other people depend on you?

Respect
Do you allow other people to be different?

Responsibility
Can others depend on you to do what you say you will do?

Questioning *your values* *cont*

Self-discipline

Can you choose the right thing even when the wrong thing is more appealing?

Steadfastness

Can you be firm in what you believe in?

Strength

Can you keep going even when others are against you?

Tact

Do you try not to hurt other people's feelings?

Thankfulness

Are you able to show that you are grateful when others are helpful or generous?

Tolerance

Can you accept differences in other people's thoughts or actions?

Thoughtfulness

Do you think of how to make others happy without being asked?

Trustworthiness

Can others rely on you to do the right thing?

Truthfulness

Do you always tell the truth?

Values: A Programme for Primary Schools ISBN 978-184590082-3

Values Education

SECTION 2

SPECIFIC VALUES ACTIVITIES

This section includes activities and work sheets designed to enable students to recognise and understand the worth of specific values.

Lower primary

Upper primary or for more able students

Confidence

Introduction

CONFIDENCE – being sure of yourself.

- On the board write the word **CONFIDENCE**.
- Discuss with students what it means.

Confidence means being sure of yourself.

- Talk to students about times when we feel confident that we can do certain things and times when we do not feel confident.

Would you feel confident doing the following things?

riding a bicycle
picking up a snake
riding a wild horse
patting a tiger on the head
drawing a picture
driving a car
riding a horse
being outside when it storms
cutting your mother's hair
making some toast

Walking together

- Have students find a partner. One partner closes their eyes. The other partner takes this person's hand and begins to lead them on a walk around the school ground. The guide's job is to make sure their partner is safe at all times. After a while get the students to swap roles and partners. Ask them to discuss if they felt confident all the time. Did they feel more confident with one person than another?
- Read *Little Red Riding Hood* to the students. Ask them to discuss whether she felt confident when she spoke to the wolf whom she thought was her grandmother. Have students brainstorm the times they don't feel confident.
- What things can destroy your confidence?

Confidence

Your personality is like a snowflake

If you looked at snowflakes under a microscope, you would see that they are made up of hexagons and triangles, with fragile, feathery spokes. Of all the billions of snowflakes that fall each year, no two the same have ever been found – scientists must have a lot of time on their hands to be able to check things like that. This individuality does not seem unusual when you realise that of all the people in the world, as far as is known, no two have the same fingerprints – not even identical twins. You are unique. No other person alive today, or who ever lived, or who ever will live, could have a thumbprint exactly like yours – or so it seems anyway. This is a simplistic way of looking at your uniqueness, but you can extend it from there. You can accept that because you are unique, nobody else will react or think exactly like you. So you have a chance to make your distinct mark on this world.

From *Make Your Own Rainbow* by Leonard Ryzman

1 Being confident helps you achieve things in life.

If the following people had not had the confidence and belief in their own ability, how might the world be different today?

a Thomas Edison ______________________________

b John Logie Baird ______________________________

c Captain James Cook ______________________________

d Louis Pasteur ______________________________

2 How confident do you feel in the following situations? Use this scale.

1 = very confident	**2 = fairly confident**
3 = not very confident	**4 = not confident at all**

a performing in a play _____

b walking into a crowded room _____

c doing maths exercises _____

d reading aloud in class _____

e doing a spelling test _____

f writing a story _____

g giving a report to the whole class _____

h swimming _____

Values: A Programme for Primary Schools ISBN 978-184590082-3

Confidence

When we are feeling good about ourselves we feel healthier, we have more energy and therefore we feel **confident**.

The Confidence Wall

Colour red the bricks that tell things that help our confidence. Colour grey the bricks that tell things that hurt our confidence.

1 I can kick a ball further than anyone in the school.	2 People say nasty things about me.	3 Monique told me that I had a great sense of humour.
4 Shiama said my new glasses look cool.	5 Javier reckons I'm great to be with on school camp.	6 Everyone is prettier than I am.
7 Classmates call me Dorky or Duck Face.	8 Theo told me he really liked the story I wrote.	9 Imran said I am always making stupid mistakes.
10 Bruno asked me if he could be my best friend.	11 I'm really dumb at mathematics.	12 "You're the best at drawing pictures of horses in the whole school," Joanne said.

Values: A Programme for Primary Schools ISBN 978-184590082-3 © 2008 Blake Education and Crown House Publishing

Caring

Introduction

CARING – showing concern and thoughtfulness towards others.

- Explain to students that **caring** means to show concern and thoughtfulness towards others.

- Ask students to name people and objects they care about, e.g. parents, siblings, classmates, pets etc.

- Ask students to write a paragraph entitled:

  "How I go about caring for ________________"
  They add the name of an object or pet.

- Ask students to consider the question, "Do I care about myself?"

  In what ways do you take care of yourself?
  What might happen if you don't take care of yourself?

  The discussion can lead into positive and negative behaviours and healthy and unhealthy choices in life.
  Why do students who can't do something say, "I don't care!"?

- What are some ways we can show those people in our community and other parts of the world that we care for them. e.g. overseas aid, Oxfam, The Salvation Army, Red Cross.

- Why are some people and things we care about more important to us than others?

- Have students make up short plays in which people demonstrate how they care in the following situations:

  - a child falls over in the playground and is hurt
  - one of your class wins an award for sport
  - a new boy who can't speak much English, comes to our school.

Caring

Things that happen to other people might make you happy, sad or uncaring. How would the things listed below make you feel?

Draw a ☺ in front of things that would make you happy.

Draw a ☹ in front of things that would make you sad.

Draw a 😐 in front of things that would not matter to you.

______ **1** your best friend gets a new bicycle

______ **2** your brother wins the school singing competition

______ **3** your mate is elected captain

______ **4** a classmate you don't like is rushed to hospital

______ **5** your mother gets a better job

______ **6** your teacher gives a classmate you don't like a special present

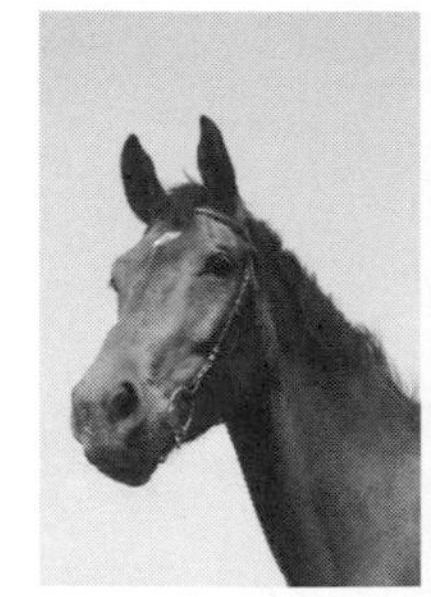

______ **7** a classmate you don't like is punished for bullying

______ **8** your classmates are given a detention for misbehaving

______ **9** a girl in your class has her lunch money stolen

______ **10** a football team member is not allowed to play because he has a cold

______ **11** your teacher has an accident in her car

______ **12** your cousin is given her own horse

______ **13** your best friend is the star of the football team

______ **14** your mother is tired and upset

Caring

In each picture fill in the speech balloon with words that show you care.

Values: A Programme for Primary Schools ISBN 978-1845900823

Kindness

Introduction

KINDNESS – being good-natured, sympathetic and kind-hearted.

- Ask students to think of a definition for **kindness**.
- Read the following story to the students.

Ryan went to watch his favourite football team play. It was a very special day for him because it was the first time he had ever been to the huge stadium in the city.

The stadium was packed with people. Ryan soon found himself seated behind a very large man. He could not see a thing. He stood up but the people behind him became angry and yelled at him to sit. Ryan felt very disappointed.

The large person in front of him suddenly turned around. He saw what Ryan's predicament was. He told Ryan to swap with him. Ryan gladly accepted. Now Ryan could see the match clearly. At half-time the man bought Ryan a can of drink and a burger.

After a few years Ryan had forgotten the details of the match but said, "I will always remember the man who was so kind to me."

- Have students tell and write stories about special deeds of kindness.
- Have each pupil describe something he or she has done recently that was kind.
- Have students brainstorm the ways they can be kind to newcomers to the school.

Kindness

Have you ever read the fables of Aesop? This one tells of kindness.

One day a lion caught a mouse. The lion held the mouse in his gigantic paw and was just about to eat it when the mouse cried out nervously, "Oh great lion could you not find the kindness in your heart to let me go? I will only make a tiny morsel and perhaps one day I could repay you."

The lion smiled. "Yes, you are right. You are so small I would hardly taste you, so I will let you go, but I just don't know how a tiny creature like you would ever be able to help me," said the King of Beasts. And with that the mouse ran away. "You are very kind," he called back to the lion.

Some time later, the great lion was struggling helplessly in a rope trap placed across a path in the jungle by hunters. No matter how much the great beast struggled he could not break the cords that held him. He was resigned to his fate, when the same mouse he had let go, came passing by. When the mouse saw the lion's predicament it wasted no time in gnawing through the ropes. Soon the lion was free and escaped before the cruel hunters returned.

"Now it is my turn to thank you for your kindness," said the grateful lion.

1 Did the lion really believe the tiny mouse could repay his kindness?

____

2 Tick the one you consider the kindest.

a ☐ a celebrity or sportsperson who visits sick children in hospital but rings the newspaper first to tell them to come with a camera

b ☐ a multimillionaire who donates money to a charity only if they are able to claim the donation as a tax deduction

c ☐ a girl who lends her coloured pencils to a classmate who has lost their own

3 When you are kind to others do you expect something in return? Discuss this with your classmates.

4 Are **love** and **kindness** the same? Write a sentence saying whether you agree or disagree and explain why. ______________________________

____

5 Discuss the differences in meanings of each of the following pairs of sentences;

a He is a funny, kind boy. / He is a funny kind of boy.

b I know you're kind. / I know your kind.

c Sally is a pretty kind girl. / Sally is a pretty, kind girl.

6 "To give is better than to receive." How could this possibly be true? Discuss it with your classmates.

THE KINGDOM OF KINDNESS

Colour red the boxes that describe something kind.
Colour grey the boxes that are not kind.

Trevor hit his sister.

Rosalind pulled a thorn out of the puppy's paw.

Mike asked his mother if she needed help with the baby.

Sharon shared her lunch with Bernie who had forgotten his.

Simone gave her teacher a bunch of flowers.

Stacey said Helen could not borrow her old pencils.

Pasqualie kicked the little kid's ball into the water.

Paul let the others play with his football.

Susan cut the lawn for her neighbour.

Joe lent Mark some lunch money.

John opened the door for Mr Smith.

Jack made a cup of tea for the workers.

Lynda invited Chan to stay at her home.

Jika tore up Lynn's story.

Values: A Programme for Primary Schools ISBN 978-184590082-3

Helpfulness

Introduction

HELPFULNESS – being unselfish and always ready to assist and share with others.

- On the board write the word **HELPFULNESS**.
- Ask students to describe what it means.
- Have students act out how they could be helpful in the following situations.
  - **a** A lady wants to know the way to the nearest post office.
  - **b** A man wants to know where he can buy some nails.
  - **c** A friend's bike has a flat tyre.
  - **d** A classmate has lost her coloured pencils.
- A person joked, "Billy is very helpful – he helps himself to this and helps himself to that!"
  What do you think the person really meant about Billy being helpful?
- Have students describe a time they have been helpful to someone in the last week.
- Ask students how the following people are helpful in our community.
  Doctors, mechanics, programmers, authors, dentists, disc jockeys
- Not only humans are helpful. Ask students to describe how these dogs are helpful to people.
  German Shepherd, Labrador, Blood Hound, St Bernard, Beagle e.g. guard dog, sniffer dog at airports, tracking dog, guide dog, companion dog, sheepdog etc.

Helpfulness

Read the story then complete the activities below.

A postman's message changes Harry's life

Harry Dola had contracted pneumonic fever at seventeen and became badly crippled. His hands were twisted, his arms and legs were thin, and the formerly active teenager was confined to a homemade wheelchair. Each day, his parents left his lunch on a nearby table before going to their factory jobs. Harry was alone all day, and once while reaching for his lunch, he fell out of the wheelchair and writhed on the floor. The disheartened young man believed he was useless – useless and seventeen. Finally, the postman came along and responded to Harry's call for help. The extra message he was given that day was, in Harry's words, "The greatest thing ever said to me". The postman's advice was "Harry, your body is crippled, but don't let the mind get crippled. Be strong in your mind".

This statement aroused powerful emotions in Harry. Had he been a different kind of person, he might simply have experienced those emotions and then forgotten about them. But because there was within him a strong core of determination to better himself, he used those new emotions in a dynamic way. He decided to make greeting cards, and painstakingly designed a few which were bought by kindly friends. Harry then established a greeting card business, and his parents put a mortgage on the house, enabling him to buy enough material for twelve thousand cards. "Harry, we are ruined if we do not sell them," said his mother. Harry replied, "Don't worry. My mind is not crippled and according to my mind, it will be done".

He actually sold nineteen thousand cards, and in time became a major manufacturer of greeting cards in the United States, even owning his own aeroplane. He also played the pipe organ, and with those twisted fingers produced music that could move you to tears.

From *Make Your Own Rainbow* by Leonard Ryzman

1 What was the helpful advice the postman gave Harry?

2 What had happened that made Harry feel useless?

3 Has anyone ever given you helpful advice that made a difference? (Think about your parents, teachers and friends.)

4 What advice would you give to the following people?
Treany – "I want to earn money to buy my mother a birthday present."
Marcus – "How can I do better at mathematics?"
Sid – "How can I be better liked by other people."
Murphy – "I'm lonely. How can I get a friend?"

Helpfulness

People can help others in many ways.

Study the pictures carefully then explain the person's actions.

Why is Myra dabbing her friend's cheeks?

Why is Nathaniel opening the door?

Why is Mary doing the dishes?

Why is Chan giving the wallet to the policeman?

Honesty

Introduction

HONESTY – being truthful and sincere at all times.

- What does being honest mean? Discuss. Have students suggest some meanings for **honesty**.

- Write these on the board.
  - Being honest means you don't steal things.
  - Being honest means you don't tell lies.
  - Being honest means you are trustworthy.

- Read *Pinocchio*. Have the students suggest consequences of telling lies.

- Students discuss what is meant by the saying "Honesty is the best policy."

- Encourage students to role-play situations where an individual's honesty is tested. e.g. Some classmates dare another to steal something from the teacher's table.

- Write the following words on the board. Have students decide on prefixes that make the opposite or negative values.

honesty	fairness	friendliness	courteous	considerate	reliable
loyalty	respect	truthfulness	tolerance	responsible	kindness

- Students describe ways they have been honest.

- Have you ever told a lie? What happened?

- Some convicts were transported because they were starving and had no money, which led to them stealing. Were these people dishonest?

Honesty

Answer this questionnaire **honestly**. Remember the answers are private to you. They are not to be read with classmates. It is given just for you to think about this important value.

Have you ever:

1 taken money that did not belong to you?
2 lied to your parents or teachers by denying that you did something?
3 blamed a classmate or friend for doing something bad when it was really you who did it?

4 lied to your parents about being too sick to go to school?
5 cheated on a test by copying answers from a classmate?
6 told your parents you didn't have homework when you really did?
7 borrowed something from a friend and deliberately not returned it?
8 received too much change from a shopkeeper and not told them?
9 ridden on public transport without paying a fare?
10 borrowed books from a library and kept them by telling people that you lost them?
11 cheated when playing sport or board games with classmates?
12 when given money to buy something said it was dearer than it really was and then kept the difference?
13 lied to others that your family is very rich?
14 told someone you liked them when you really didn't?
15 lied about yourself so other students would think you're cool and want you as their friend?
16 sneaked into a movie or event without paying?
17 taken things from the classroom that didn't belong to you?
18 found something valuable but made no attempt to return it to its owner?
19 damaged something belonging to another and then just put it back without saying anything?
20 eaten sweets that belonged to someone else?

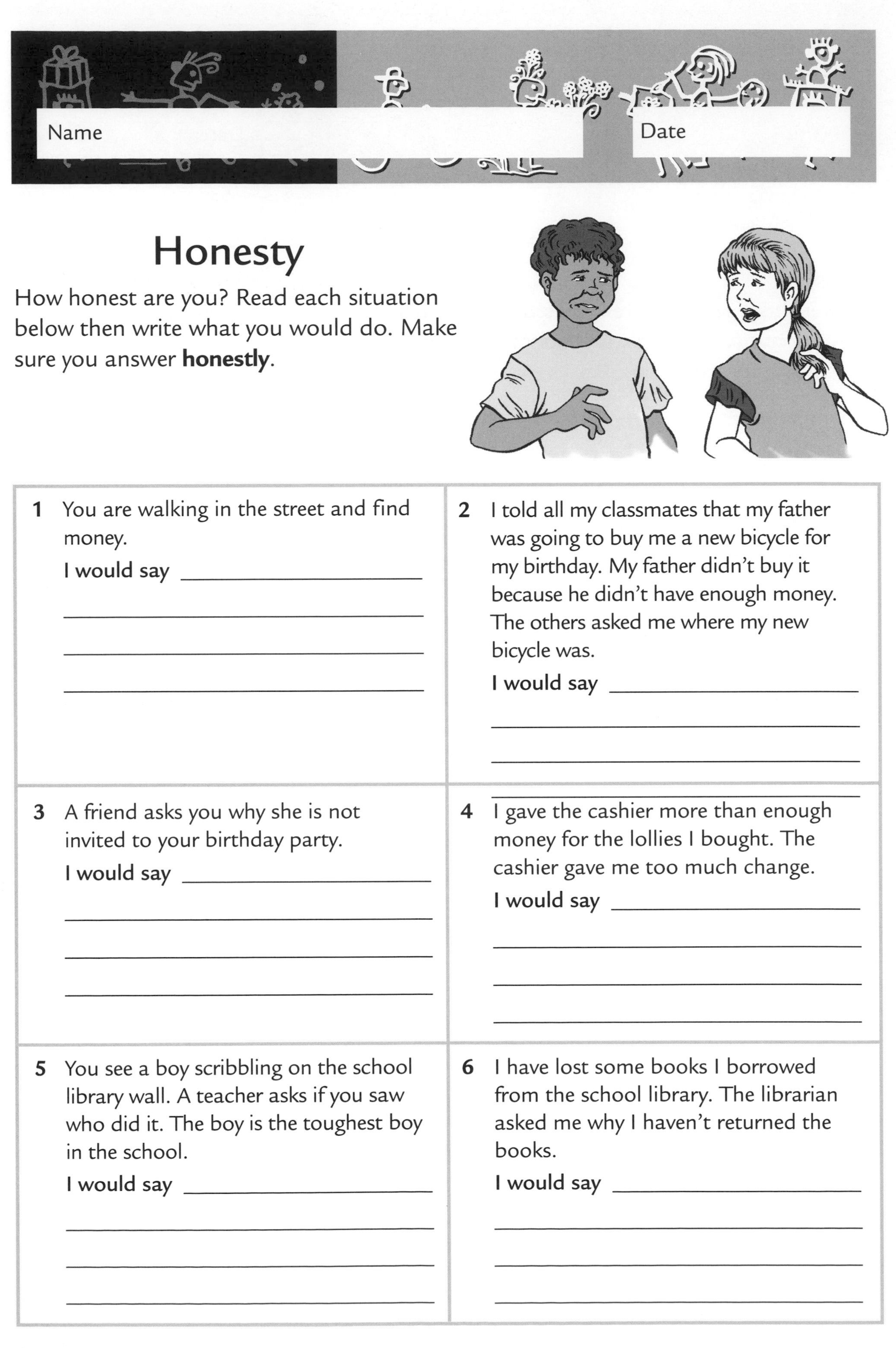

Name Date

Honesty

How honest are you? Read each situation below then write what you would do. Make sure you answer **honestly**.

1 You are walking in the street and find money. **I would say** ____________________	**2** I told all my classmates that my father was going to buy me a new bicycle for my birthday. My father didn't buy it because he didn't have enough money. The others asked me where my new bicycle was. **I would say** ____________________
3 A friend asks you why she is not invited to your birthday party. **I would say** ____________________	**4** I gave the cashier more than enough money for the lollies I bought. The cashier gave me too much change. **I would say** ____________________
5 You see a boy scribbling on the school library wall. A teacher asks if you saw who did it. The boy is the toughest boy in the school. **I would say** ____________________	**6** I have lost some books I borrowed from the school library. The librarian asked me why I haven't returned the books. **I would say** ____________________

Values: A Programme for Primary Schools ISBN 978-184590082-3 © 2008 Blake Education and Crown House Publishing

Courage

Introduction

COURAGE – meeting dangers and difficulties firmly and without fear.

- Discuss with students what is meant by the word **courage**.
- Students consider if it is OK to be afraid in certain situations. Have them explain the times they may be afraid, e.g. going to the dentist, being alone in the dark, when an adult gets angry with you, thunder and lightning, spiders.
- Read the following story to the students.

> Azim Hafeez was born without any fingers on his right hand, but he still wanted to play top level cricket as a fast bowler for his country, Pakistan. You might think he could play at a lower level, but international cricket? I saw part of the 1983 series in Australia where Azim turned the ball and took the wickets to become Pakistan's number one fast bowler, missing fingers and all. He felt so strongly that he could make it in the big league, he simply would not settle for less. He is now an inspiration to young children in a similar position.

- What kind of courage did Azim Hafeez possess to achieve what he did?
- Have students create role-play situations in which people display acts of courage.
- Ask students to name occupations that are dangerous and which take courage to do, e.g. a firefighter.

Courage

Have you ever been afraid? Below is a list of fears many of us have. **Tick** the ones you have.

At the end **rate** your fears **1** or **2**. (1 is a very scary thing for you, while 2 might only scare you a little bit.) **Colour** the box.

- ☐ when the weather is thunder and lightning 1 2
- ☐ when I meet new adults 1 2
- ☐ when I see an accident 1 2
- ☐ when someone grabs me unexpectedly 1 2
- ☐ when my parents argue 1 2
- ☐ when a large, savage dog is barking at me 1 2
- ☐ when I am alone in the dark 1 2
- ☐ when I have to visit the dentist or the doctor 1 2
- ☐ when the teacher is angry or disappointed with my behaviour 1 2
- ☐ when I am a passenger in a speeding car 1 2
- ☐ when older students threaten me 1 2
- ☐ when I have to stand in front of the whole class and give a report 1 2

Describe something else that you are afraid of.

____

____

____

Courage

How courageous are you? Briefly explain what you would do in the following situations.

1 You are home alone on a dark night. Suddenly you hear a noise outside.	**5** You are riding in the back seat of a car and suddenly you see a large truck racing towards you on the wrong side of the road.
2 You are walking home after school by yourself when a group of older, bigger children challenge you to a fight.	**6** You are at the doctor's surgery when the doctor says, "I'm going to give you a needle to help you get better."
3 The dentist, after looking in your mouth, says "I'm going to have to pull two teeth out".	**7** You are in your bedroom when you see a large spider crawling across the floor.
4 You are in your bed at night when you hear your parents having a very loud argument.	**8** You are with a group of friends in a boat when they challenge you to swim to some nearby rocks. You know there are jellyfish in the ocean.

Values: A Programme for Primary Schools ISBN 978-1845900823

Respect

Introduction

RESPECT – recognising the worth, quality and importance of others despite their differences.

- Have students discuss what is meant by **respect.** Ask them to describe simple ways in which they can demonstrate respect to others.

- In small groups students compile lists of things they can do to show that they respect others.

- Discuss with students why manners are important in everyday life. If there were no standard manners, what kind of world would it be?

- Have students consider courtesy practised in other countries as a sign of respect, e.g. Japan - bowing to guests; France - greeting people by kissing both cheeks.

- Discuss the reasons why many acts of courtesy are now disappearing, e.g. opening a door for elders, offering a woman a seat on a bus.

- Have students role-play stories they have made up in which a person demonstrates respectful or disrespectful behaviour.

  Examples
  - A crowded bus - a pregnant lady is standing.
  - You are waiting in a queue to be served when a person deliberately pokes fun at another person who is wearing traditional clothing from another country.

Respect

Read the following story.

A man once opened a door for a woman. "Hmmph!" she snapped. "I suppose you opened the door because I'm a woman, and you think I am not capable of doing so myself."

"Not at all," replied the man cheerily. "I opened the door because I am a gentleman and courteous to all people!"

1 Describe when you have displayed respect to another in the last week.

____

____

____

2 Make a list of things you might do to show others that you are a respectful person, e.g. listen carefully while the teacher is talking.

____

____

3 Colour blue the boxes that show respectful behaviour. Colour red the boxes that show disrespectful behaviour.

push others out of line	wait your turn	say please and thank you
listen while others talk	barge in front of others	share your sweets
making fun of someone's name	help those in difficulty	talk over others

4 Last week, a parent gave up their time to organise a sports day for your class. It was a very enjoyable day. Write a short note thanking them on behalf of the class.

____

____

____

____

Respect

In the balloons write what a respectful person would say or do.

Values: A Programme for Primary Schools ISBN 978-184590082-3

Fairness

Introduction

FAIRNESS – being open-minded and completely free from bias or injustice.

- Discuss with students what **fairness** means. Have them describe fair and unfair experiences.

- Students form small groups to prepare role-plays that demonstrate fairness in action. e.g. Two boys are found fighting in the yard. The teacher must punish both. Billy claims that Tommy began the fight but Tommy has a bleeding nose. The teacher's punishment must be fair.

- Why is it important for the following people to be fair? What might happen if they were not fair?

  referee parent teacher judge

- Ask students to discuss what they think are fair consequences for other students who:
  - deliberately scribble on school walls.
  - bully younger students.
  - 'mess about' when the teacher leaves the room.
  - push smaller students out of the tuckshop queues.

- Discuss with students the need to have certain rights but also the responsibilities that come with them.

  For example:
  Joanne has the right to express her opinions but is it fair when she hurts the feelings of others?
  Mr Brown has the right to own a car but is it fair if he drives it recklessly?

Fairness

1 Read this story then complete the exercises below.

Two fishermen once had a bitter argument over some juicy oysters they had found in the bay. Each man claimed that he should keep them. After a long argument, they both finally agreed they should get a friend to decide who owned them and thus settle their dispute.

They went to their friend's house and explained their dilemma. The friend asked the first man why he felt the oysters were his.

"Well," replied the man, "we used my boat to get to the spot where the oyster bed is so therefore they all belong to me!"

"And you?" asked the friend glancing in the direction of the second man.

"I should keep all the oysters because it was me who risked his life and dived for them and gathered them from the ocean bed."

When they had both finished, the friend thought deeply for a moment. "I have made a decision," he said. He left the table and returned with a knife and fork. Using the knife he opened each oyster and then with the fork he scooped up the juicy flesh and ate them all.

The two fishermen were surprised and yelled, "That's not fair!"

When he had finished, the friend turned to the men and said, "My decision was very fair. Neither of you gained and neither of you lost."

1 Do you think the friend's judgement was fair? Explain.

____

____

2 Imagine you are a teacher. Make a fair judgement for each of the following.

a A small boy complains that a bigger boy knocked his ice-cream cone onto the dirt. The bigger boy tells you it was an accident.

____

____

b A girl claims a classmate has stolen her video game. The other girl says her mother bought it for her and she must take it home after school.

____

____

The Fairness Tree

Colour green those decisions that are fair.

Colour yellow those decisions you think are unfair.

Loyalty

Introduction

LOYALTY –being faithful to your promises, responsibilities or undertakings.

- Discuss with students the meaning of **loyalty**. Have them suggest their own ideas of what it means.

- Write the following on the board.

  ONLY A FRIEND CAN BETRAY YOU

  Discuss its meaning.

- Students describe their own experiences of when they displayed loyalty or when someone was loyal to them.

- Students form small groups and create and role-play stories of loyalty.

- Play the record *Two Little Boys* by Rolf Harris. Have them discuss the loyalty the boys showed to each other.

- Have the students access the library to find stories that illustrate loyalty. (Aesop's Fables may be good ones to start with.)

- Students brainstorm all the qualities that a friend should have.

- Ask the students to consider why loyalty is something often mentioned on Remembrance Day.

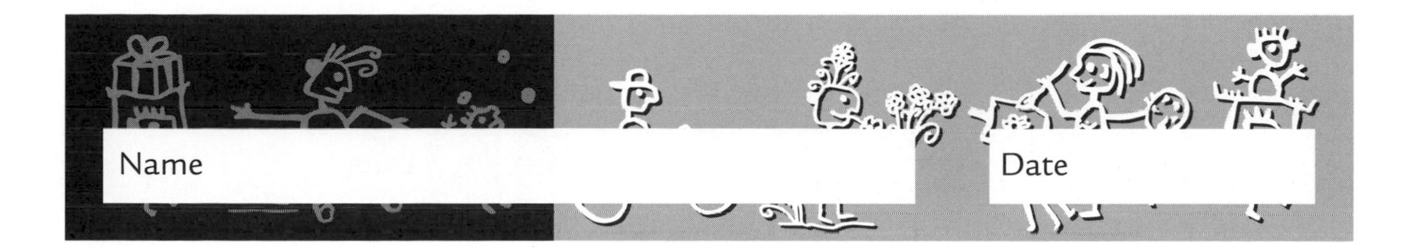

Loyalty

1 Read this story.

Twenty young naval officers stood rigidly to attention in a perfectly straight line on the wharf. They were being addressed by their commanding officer.

"I want five volunteers," began the commanding officer solemnly. "It is for a very dangerous mission and it is highly probable that those who volunteer will not return. For this reason I will not demand you make an immediate decision. I want you to think about it carefully. I will return to the building over there and while I'm away I want volunteers to take one step forward."

The officer returned to the building and after 15 minutes emerged once again. He marched towards the men. Much to his disappointment all the men were still standing to attention in a straight line.

"I understand," he said quietly, "but I thought that your loyalty to your country may have persuaded some of you to volunteer."

It was only later that he found out that the straight line was caused by all the men taking one step forward.

2 Describe a situation that illustrates loyalty towards another.

____

____

____

3 We expect a friend to be loyal. How could you show you were loyal to your friends? e.g. I would stick up for them when they are in trouble.

____

4 People express their loyalty to a country by singing the national anthem proudly. What is another way we can show loyalty to our country?

____

5 Play this game. Find a partner. Your partner closes their eyes while you take them on a walk around the schoolyard. You must make sure your partner does not bump into anything or fall. This whole activity is to be done without talking. After 10 minutes swap places with your partner.

Loyalty

Look at the following. Tick **Yes** or **No**. Give reasons for your answers. Share your answers with your classmates.

Can they be loyal?

1 Can a girl be loyal?

☐ Yes ☐ No

Why? ______________________________

____

2 Can a teacher be loyal?

☐ Yes ☐ No

Why? ______________________________

____

3 Can a younger brother be loyal?

☐ Yes ☐ No

Why? ______________________________

____

4 Can a very poor, homeless person be loyal?

☐ Yes ☐ No

Why? ______________________________

____

5 Can a boy be loyal?

☐ Yes ☐ No

Why? ______________________________

____

6 Can a snake be loyal?

☐ Yes ☐ No

Why? ______________________________

____

Responsibility

■ Introduction

RESPONSIBILITY – being able to account for all your deeds and actions.

- Have students suggest what they think the word **responsibility** means.
- Students form small groups. Have them brainstorm all the responsibilities they have at school. These should be recorded on large charts.

Example **<u>Our responsibilities</u>**

We are responsible for keeping our room tidy.
We are responsible for looking after our books.

- In small groups students make mind maps about responsibility – at school, at home, at play etc.

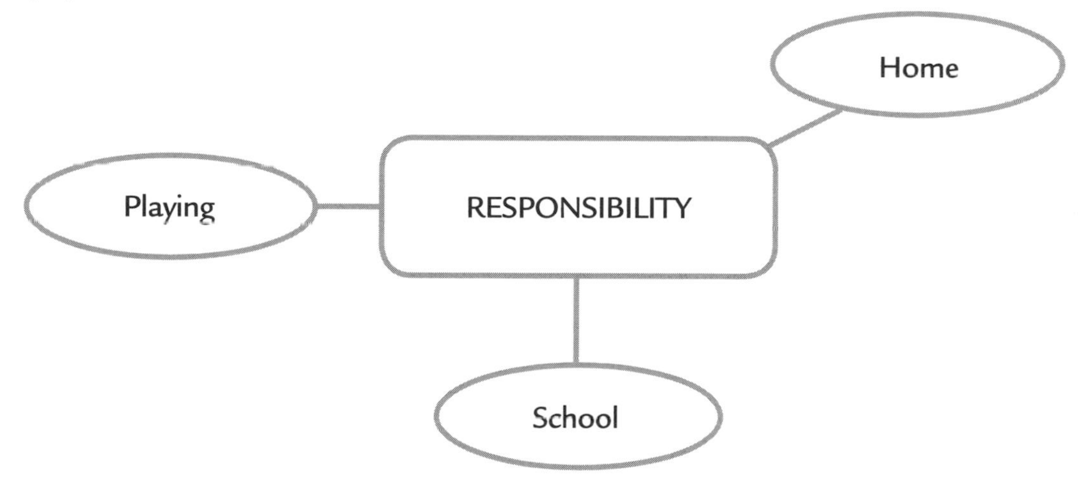

- Explain to students that everyone has certain rights. However with these rights come responsibilities. Students consider the following.
  - We have the right to own cars, but have we the right to drive dangerously?
  - We have the right to have money, but does this give us the right to steal?

Responsibility

1 Read the story then complete the activities below.

Jill and Jack wanted a puppy. They pestered their mother for many weeks. Their mother said, "If I allow you to have a puppy you must care for it every day".

"Of course we will," replied the children.

Some weeks later their mother took them to a local pet store that had puppies for sale.

Jill and Jack chose a small, black and white terrier puppy. They called it Sniffy.

Each day Jill's job was to fill up his water dish. Jack's job was to make sure that he had food to eat. They took turns at taking Sniffy for a walk in the park.

One day, six months later, the children's mother came home tired from work. The two children were inside watching television. As she walked along the garden path she heard Sniffy whining. He seemed lonely. When she looked, his water dish and food dish were both empty.

"Why hasn't Sniffy been fed and given fresh water?" asked the children's mother. "And why don't you spend time playing with him or taking him for a walk? He hasn't been walked for a long time."

"We're too tired," groaned the children.

2 Read the sentences below. Find the missing words to fill the spaces.

Sniffy was whining because he was ____________ and ___________. He felt ___________ because the children no longer played with him or took him for a __________. Sally and Jack were ___________ that they had been so ____________ and ____________. Sniffy taught the two students that they must be ____________.

Word Bank

sorry walk
hungry lazy
responsible
unloved
careless
thirsty

3 What does **responsible** mean?

____

4 Write two things for which you are responsible:

a at school. ____

b at home. ____

Values: A Programme for Primary Schools ISBN 978-1845900823

Responsibility

Describe the responsibilities each person now has.

1 George has just been given a new bicycle by his Uncle Harry. __________ __________ __________	**2** Shona has just been appointed as teacher of a Year 3 class. __________ __________ __________
3 Timothy has been given a kitten. __________ __________ __________	**4** Eremin has just borrowed some books from the library. __________ __________ __________
5 Mitchell has been left in charge of the class while Miss Smailela goes to the office. __________ __________ __________	**6** Mr Yang is the proud owner of a new sports car. __________ __________ __________
7 Mrs Belldood has just been made manager of the supermarket. __________ __________ __________	**8** Mr Karoubas has left Mariah in charge of his vegetable garden while he is away on holidays. __________ __________ __________

Values: A Programme for Primary Schools ISBN 978-1845900823

Friendliness

Introduction

FRIENDLINESS – being kind and welcoming to all others.

- Have students suggest what they think the words **friend**, **friendship** and **friendliness** mean.

- Students form small groups to discuss and record the ways they could be friendly to a newly-arrived classmate.

e.g.
- We could show them where the toilet block and art room are.
- We could ask them to sit with us at lunchtime.

- Discuss with students what being a friend means. Ask questions such as: Can a parent be a friend? Can a brother be a friend?

- Students brainstorm the qualities that make a good friend, e.g. loyalty, helpfulness.

- Ask students to consider the following carefully:

Is it better to have one true friend or lots of friends?

- Have students discuss the following:

What is a fair-weather friend?
A friend in need is a friend indeed.

- Students write and describe a special friend. They are not to name that person. The other students must guess the person described.

Friendliness

1 Are you a good friend? Tick the points you feel are important in a friend. Cross those you feel are not important.

- **a** ☐ someone who can keep a secret
- **b** ☐ someone who plays fair in games
- **c** ☐ someone who likes to show off
- **d** ☐ someone who stands up for me
- **e** ☐ someone who helps me
- **f** ☐ someone who can run faster than all our classmates
- **g** ☐ someone who likes me even when I grizzle or bite my fingernails
- **h** ☐ someone who doesn't care if I do something better than he or she can
- **i** ☐ someone who is good at telling jokes
- **j** ☐ someone who likes some of the things I like
- **k** ☐ someone who buys things for me at the tuckshop
- **l** ☐ someone who always tells others that I'm a great kid
- **m** ☐ someone who is good at sport

2 Now think about a friend. Put a star beside those traits which your friend has.

3 Mark the traits you have with a ◆.

4 Are you really a good friend? Think about it and about some things you could do to be a better friend.

The friendly forest

Colour green the leaves that tell how we can show others we are friendly.
Colour brown the leaves that contain unfriendly things.

Pride

Introduction

PRIDE – having a positive opinion of your own worth and being proud of your achievements.

- Begin by explaining to students some things that have made you feel proud.

  Example:
  - When I was at school I felt very proud when my teacher said I was trying really hard.
  - I felt proud when I made the netball team.
  - I felt proud when my first baby was born.

- Now ask students to share things about themselves that make them feel proud.

- Students sit in small groups, close their eyes and think of something they did that has made them feel proud. "Can you remember a time you did something or achieved something that made you feel proud of yourself? Can you remember how you felt? Did you tell anyone else you felt proud? If you did, can you remember what they said?"

- Some students, especially those with low self-esteem, do not claim to have ever tasted success, so therefore they have nothing to be proud of.

  Prod these students with appropriate questions such as:
  You can ride a bike to school. Can you remember when you first learnt to ride it? Did you feel proud of that achievement?

- Distribute sheets of half-size A4 paper to the students. On each page they write something they are proud of. The pages should be stapled together to make a pupil PRIDE book.

- Discuss with students why they feel proud to be from their country. Have individual students explain why their country is such a good country to live in.

My Pride Flags

In the flags write something you, or someone else, has done that has made you proud.

e.g. I feel proud when I get most of my maths correct.
I am proud because my little brother can do up his shoelaces.

Decorate each flag.

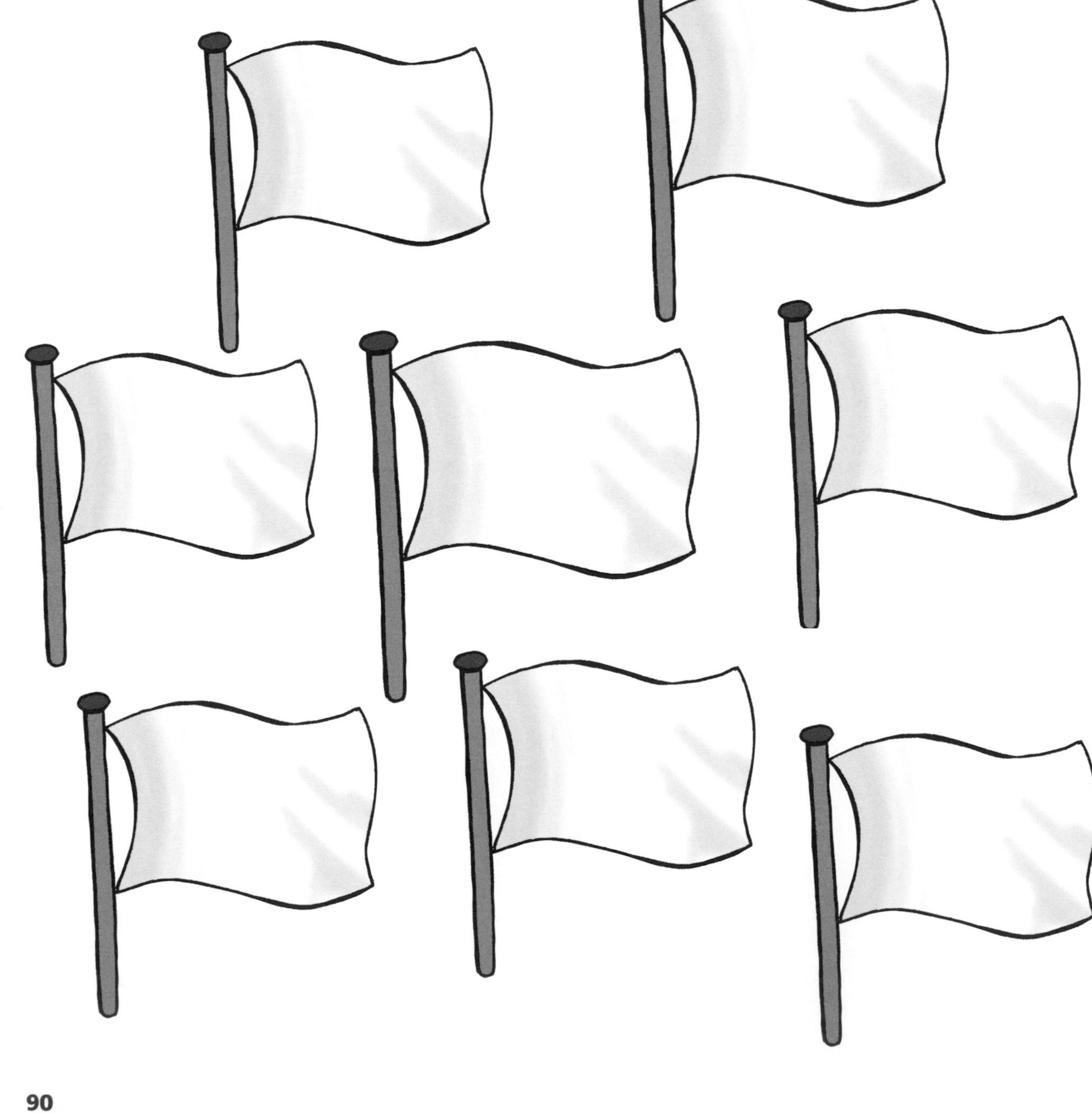

My Pledge

To express pride in their country people often make a pledge.
Colour in the letters of this pledge and decorate the border.

I AM PROUD TO BE

______________.

I WILL HONOUR AND RESPECT OUR FLAG.

I WILL BE COURTEOUS AND KIND TO OTHERS.

I WILL ABIDE BY THE LAWS OF MY SCHOOL AND COMMUNITY.

In small groups make up your own pledge for your classroom.

Values: A Programme for Primary Schools ISBN 978-184590082-3

Determination

■ Introduction

***DETERMINATION** – being resolute and possessing a firmness of purpose.*

- Write the word **determination** in large letters on the board. Have students explain what they think determination means.

- Challenge students to carry out small but complex tasks.

Examples

- Fold a sheet of paper and tear it until it is in the smallest pieces possible.
- Clap their hands and count the claps for five minutes.
- Doodle on a sheet of paper.
  Who can keep going until the paper is full?
- Have students note the classmates who stick at the task.

- Tell simple, short stories of determination to students, e.g. Bruce and the Spider.

- Students write the following saying on a sheet of paper and decorate it.

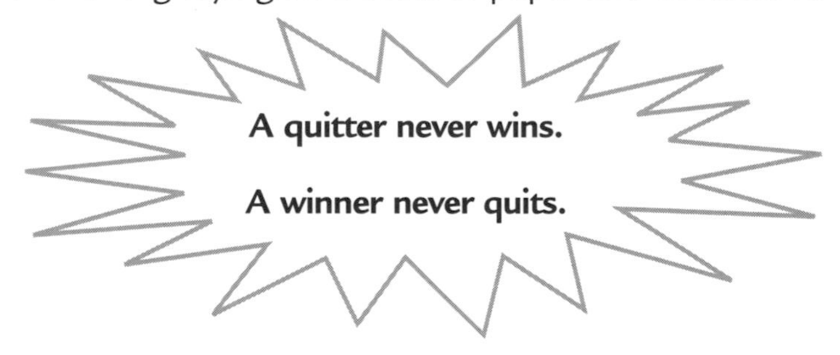

- Students form small groups and role-play stories about how someone overcame difficulties to eventually succeed.

- Have the class brainstorm all the qualities a determined person has.

- Discuss the following sayings.
  - Mistakes are an essential part of learning.
  - Show me a person who has never made a mistake, and I'll show you a person who has never learnt anything.

Determination

Read the story then complete the activities below.

What do you think makes a person a champion?

Some say it's just hard work. If a person is willing to work hard by practising and practising every day, that's all it takes.

Others say it's great coaching that makes the difference. If you've got a good coach to show you the skills, then you are bound to be a champion.

Others even say it's not hard work or coaching, it's simply a case of opportunity. If the circumstances are right in a child's life then he or she is bound to be a champion.

Many people believe that to become a champion all you need is to be born with talent or ability, while others say it's encouragement or inspiration.

However the people who really know what makes a champion agree that all the above are important, but they add there is something much more fundamental and vital to the creation of a champion and that is **desire**.

A famous athletics coach once said, "Show me a youngster with a desire to win and I'll show you a person who will practise hard the many hours it takes to become a champion".

This of course goes for all things in life. Your desire to succeed at school will no doubt determine the success you have in life.

1 What value does the author believe that a youngster must have to become a champion?

____

2 What advice would you give to someone who wanted to improve their marks in mathematics or spelling?

____

3 If a classmate was a faster runner than you, what might you do to be able to beat that person in a race?

____

4 Do you give up easily when things are tough? Think about it! Write a paragraph describing a time you could have given up but didn't.

____

____

When the going gets tough the tough get going.

5 What does this mean? Write on the back of this sheet.

Values: A Programme for Primary Schools ISBN 978-184590082-3 © 2008 Blake Education and Crown House Publishing

Determination

Here are two activities to test your determination.

1 As quickly as you can, find and colour any two numbers next to each other that add to 14.

7	3	9	5	8	6	4	9	3	11	8	6	11	3	9
2	12	7	7	14	0	8	6	3	9	11	2	4	10	5
7	8	3	5	9	8	7	8	6	3	10	4	3	11	3
7	6	0	9	5	7	7	4	9	5	6	8	5	9	5
2	4	13	1	8	4	11	14	0	7	7	6	8	4	9
7	9	5	2	5	10	3	3	7	2	8	5	9	4	2
13	1	8	11	3	6	3	12	2	6	8	3	11	3	1
6	8	5	9	3	4	3	11	6	7	9	5	10	4	0

2 This time see how quickly you can colour all the letters that follow each other in the alphabet.

Z	D	O	P	Q	F	G	T	H	I	X
V	W	B	M	N	J	K	T	U	A	B
A	B	Y	V	L	M	T	U	Z	B	C
Z	M	G	H	S	T	V	X	Y	R	S
V	W	R	T	U	E	F	Y	Z	M	T
M	J	K	N	O	X	W	P	Q	F	G
X	Y	Q	H	I	R	S	N	O	V	W
N	P	T	U	T	C	D	D	E	R	S
V	W	X	T	U	Z	Y	X	Y	M	N

Values: A Programme for Primary Schools ISBN 978-184590082-3 © 2008 Blake Education and Crown House Publishing

Purposefulness

Introduction

PURPOSEFULNESS – having the ability to achieve a desired result.

- Have students discuss what **purposeful** means. What does it mean when we hear someone say, "You did it on purpose!"

  This means it was done for a desired result.

- Students form small groups and discuss the purpose of things we do.

  Examples
  - What is the purpose of us having a birthday party?
  - What is the purpose of eating healthy foods?
  - What is the purpose of learning mathematics?

- Explain to students that when you are young it is often hard to understand the purpose of certain things.

  Examples
  - What purpose is there in learning to read?
  - What purpose is there in learning a foreign language?

- Discuss with students that having a purpose leads to success in life. Talk to them about famous people who set out to be the best at football, acting etc.

  Example
  - Albert Einstein was told by his teacher that he would never amount to anything in his life. Because he had a purpose, he became probably the greatest mathematician of all time.

Purposefulness

Read the story then complete the activities below.

The Olympic creed says: *The glory of the Olympic games is not in the victory, but in taking part.* In other words the essential thing in life is not the conquering but in the fight.

In 1956 one fine performance was by the American swimmer Shelley Mann.

When Shelley was five, she had polio so badly that she could hardly move a muscle in her body. She decided to go to a swimming pool to try to build a little strength in her feeble arms and legs. The day she first found the strength to lift an arm out of the water was a major triumph.

As she improved her strength, she set herself goals such as swimming the width of the pool. In time, and after much pain and hard work, she achieved this. Her next goal was to swim the length of the pool. In time she swam a length, two lengths, three lengths ...

So much was her desire and purpose to improve her performances that she became the greatest female swimmer of her time in America. In 1956, at the Melbourne Olympics she won gold for the butterfly, one of the most difficult strokes of all.

When she stood on the podium clasping the gold medal and wiping the tears of joy from her eyes, she realised her sense of purpose all those years ago had enabled her to succeed beyond her wildest dreams.

1 What was the purpose of the young polio-stricken girl, Shelley Mann, going to a swimming pool?

____

2 Did Shelley set out to be a champion?

____

3 Lots of things have a purpose. Write what you think the purpose of the following would be.

a good manners ____________________

b learning mathematics ____________________

c going to church ____________________

d classroom discipline ____________________

4 What is the purpose of each of the following? Discuss the consequences if they were ignored?

________________ ________________ ________________

Values: A Programme for Primary Schools ISBN 978-1845900823 © 2008 Blake Education and Crown House Publishing

Purposefulness

Explain the purpose of each.

1 The lifeguards ordered the boys to swim between the flags.	**2** My parents grounded me for going to play at my friend's home without telling them first.
3 John took a big bunch of flowers to his mother who had been feeling ill.	**4** Mrs Smith locked all the doors and windows of her home before going out for the evening.

Trustworthiness

Introduction

TRUSTWORTHINESS – being reliable and honest at all times.

- Have students discuss what is meant by **trustworthiness**. Ask them how they can show others that they are trustworthy.

- Students complete a "trust walk". One child is blindfolded and stands at the back of the classroom. A team-mate gives explicit directions to the blindfolded pupil to guide them back to their desk/table and chair. The blindfolded pupil must place their trust in the classmate's directions.

- Students discuss whether a pet, such as a dog, can be trustworthy.

  Example
  - If you put a puppy in a room full of cakes do you think the puppy would touch them?

- A guide dog is trusted fully by its owner. Have students make up stories about how humans have put their trust in dogs and other animals.

- Ask students to discuss the saying:

  He/She can never be trusted.

- You trust a teacher to teach you well, but can you be trusted not to misbehave when the teacher goes out of the classroom?

- People such as police, bank managers, teachers, pilots and nurses are said to be in a "position of trust".
  - Students discuss what these words actually mean.
  - Are there other occupations in which we must be able to trust the person in charge?

Trustworthiness

Simonetta, Lucy and Mike all belonged to the same club. Their club wanted to raise money to buy some sports equipment so they decided to help by doing odd jobs for neighbours.

One day, the three were cleaning up old Mr Jones' shed. He lived in the same street as they did. He had often helped them before by paying them for doing chores like cutting the lawn, trimming the hedge and generally tidying up.

As the three children were just finishing tidying the shed Mike noticed some old football and cricket cards in a tea chest. "Hey look at these," he gasped. "They would be worth a fortune today."

"Wow," said Lucy. "I'd love to have those. Let's take them. Old Mr Jones wouldn't know. He probably forgot about them long ago!"

"Yeah," replied Mike. "That's right, he wouldn't remember he had them and he'd never notice they were gone." Mike put some cards in his pocket.

"That's stealing," said Simonetta firmly. "Leave them there. Taking them would not only be dishonest, but would break the trust Mr Jones has for us."

"Oh, I guess you're right Simonetta," said Mike. He put the cards back.

Just then Mr Jones came into the shed. He had a tray of biscuits and three glasses of soft drink. "You youngsters have done a great job." he said. "Here's your pay and here's more money to help your club. By the way, see those old football cards in the tea chest? I haven't got any grandchildren so I would really like to give them to you."

Simonetta, Lucy and Mike looked at each other and smiled.

1 In the boxes draw a comic strip that illustrates the story.

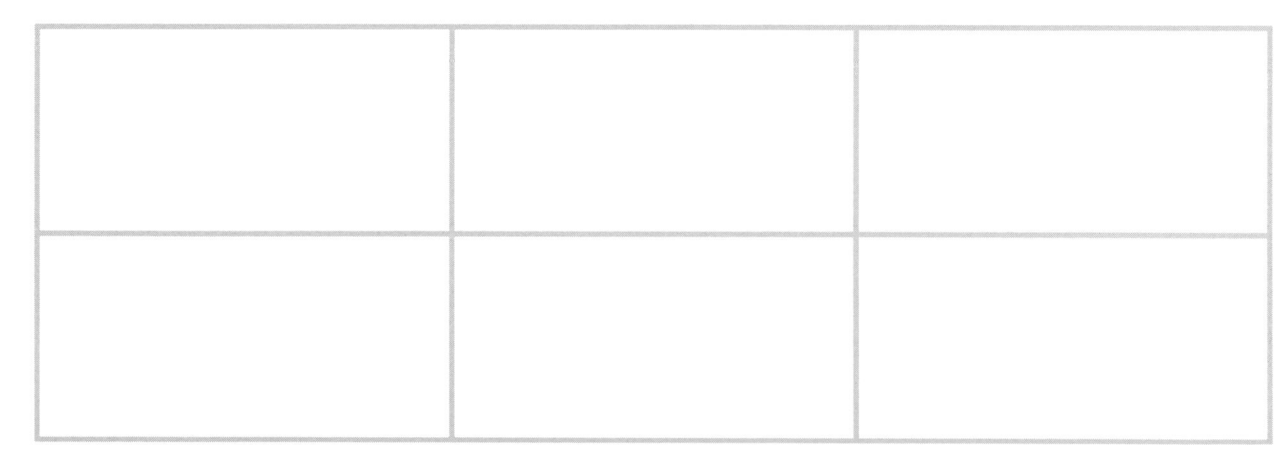

2 Why do you think some people steal? Is there any time when it is right to steal? Discuss this with your classmates.

3 Robin Hood is said to have robbed from the rich to give to the poor. Does this make robbing people correct? Conduct a class debate.

Trustworthiness

Cindy was always interested in electronics. After leaving school, she qualified as an electronics technician. Cindy decided to establish her own business. This was expensive and she had to borrow a lot of money from the bank. However she was determined to succeed.

Six months later, business was not good. Sometimes she was late making repayments on her loan, and she was continually pestered by other creditors demanding money she owed them for supplies and materials.

One day, a man entered her store carrying a DVD player. “I would like you to fix this,” he said. When he saw no one else was about, he began to talk in a lower voice. “Look, I work for a large electrical goods store and we always need lots of electrical goods repaired. I’ve got a deal. I’ll make sure the company gets all the repairs done here. You can add more money to your account and then you and I will split the difference. It’s so simple the owner of the company will never know and we’ll both be very rich!”

Cindy looked at the man. “I will have no part in your dishonest plan!” she said angrily. “Please leave my shop and take your DVD player with you. I charge all people a fair price for repairs. My good name means more to me than money.”

The man smiled. “I was really hoping you’d say that. I am actually the owner of the business and I’m sick of being ripped off by shonky repairers in this area. I’m going to put all the repairs from my chain of stores in your hands.”

Today, Cindy has a thriving business and employs a staff of four others to keep up with all the work. She does not owe the bank anything and has even been able to purchase her own premises.

1 This story illustrates how Cindy was rewarded for being trustworthy. How trustworthy are you? Think about it.

2 What do we mean when we say, “They cannot be trusted”?

____

____

3 Have you ever been tempted to steal something but didn’t? Tell your classmates about your experience.

4 What people in the community do you think are the most trustworthy? Number the following from 1 to 8 in the order you think they should come. Number one is most trustworthy, number 8 the least trustworthy.

police ☐ teachers ☐ doctors ☐ strangers ☐

next-door-neighbours ☐ librarians ☐ dentists ☐ parents ☐

Values: A Programme for Primary Schools ISBN 978-184590082-3

Excellence

Introduction

EXCELLENCE - having the ability to excel and be superior.

Have students suggest meanings of the word **excellence**. Does it mean just good or does it mean better than good? Have the students write the definition above in their best writing.

- Students learn the following saying.

Good, better, best
Never let it rest
Until your good is better
And your better best.

- Ask each pupil to disclose the name of something he or she would like to be better at. Discuss with them how they can improve.

  Examples
  - Sam: I would like to do better at spelling. I can if I spend more time learning the words.
  - Jack: I would like to be better at football. I can if I practise more.

- Have students write a story about a famous person who has achieved excellence. Ask them to describe how this person was able to do so well.

Success is 10% inspiration and 90% perspiration.

- Discuss this saying with the students.

Excellence

We should all work hard to achieve excellence. Is your school an excellent place to be? How happy are you at school? Fill in the table and score yourself at the bottom of the page.

	Always	Sometimes	Never
1 I always look forward to going to school.			
2 School is a great place to be.			
3 I get on really well with all the other students in my class.			
4 The students in my class are helpful and friendly.			
5 I feel safe and happy in the playground.			
6 Students at this school invite others to join in games.			
7 There are always lots of things to do at school.			
8 We are able to eat our lunches in pleasant, comfortable surroundings.			
9 All the teachers at our school are helpful and friendly.			
10 The discipline at our school is very good.			
11 Our school keeps parents well informed as to what is happening.			
12 I am really learning a lot at school.			
13 My school organises lots of enjoyable activities outside the classroom.			
14 Troublemaking students and bad behaviour are dealt with really well at my school.			
15 The Physical Education and Library programs are excellent.			

If you answered **Always** give yourself 3 points. If you answered **Sometimes** give yourself 2 points and if you answered **Never** give yourself 1 point.

Score:
40-45 Excellent
30-39 Very Good
20-29 Good
2-19 Not really good

Values: A Programme for Primary Schools ISBN 978-184590082-3 © 2008 Blake Education and Crown House Publishing

Excellence

Colour this pattern. There is no right or wrong way however the idea is for you to produce a picture by colouring it carefully.

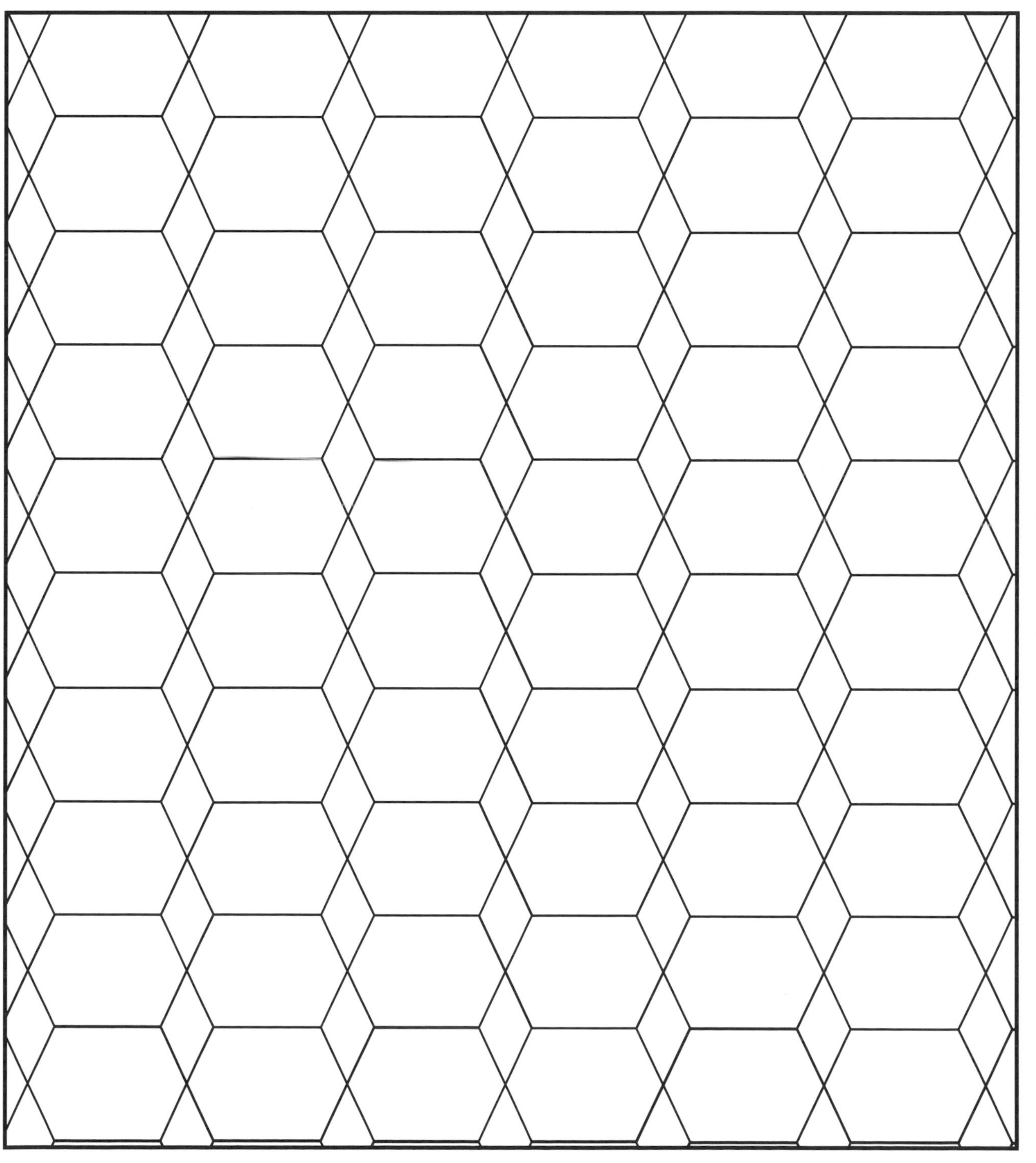

Doing your best

Introduction

***DOING YOUR BEST** – always striving to do everything to the best of your ability.*

- Discuss with students what is meant by **doing your best**.

  Have them describe times they have achieved something simply because they did their best. Ask them to write stories of these achievements under the heading:

  Winners Are Grinners

- Ask students to discuss the saying:

  There may be times when even your best is not good enough.

  When could this be true?

- In groups, students write proverbs on colourful posters and hang them in the classroom.

  Examples
  - **What's worth doing is worth doing well.**
  - **Practise makes perfect.**
  - **If at first you don't succeed, try, try again.**
  - **Cut your coat according to your cloth.**

- Students create and act out plays in which someone, perhaps a well-known person, has achieved fame simply by doing their best.

- Discuss with students what is meant by doing your best in the following situations:
  a at school
  b at home
  c on the sporting field.

Doing Your Best

1 This activity tests how well you can concentrate. Locate all the groups of three letters that directly follow each other in the alphabet, e.g. abc, mno etc. You have 3 minutes. There is no correct score. Just do your best.

Score ________

A	x	p	y	t	m	d	e	f	p	a	d	f	j	m	g	h	i	t	s	o	x	y	p	q	r	z	s
B	a	f	g	h	a	c	f	h	m	n	o	i	x	p	t	g	a	t	v	v	b	c	x	f	g	h	n
C	a	x	y	z	t	a	l	j	k	z	b	a	z	b	n	p	q	r	o	r	z	v	w	x	a	t	y
D	a	b	c	y	z	t	o	a	m	p	x	y	g	h	i	z	t	o	n	a	j	k	l	a	d	g	y
E	x	b	n	o	p	a	y	z	y	a	t	z	x	y	m	r	s	t	a	t	v	w	x	y	b	e	m
F	o	a	z	y	b	d	d	e	f	m	o	a	m	n	o	t	z	f	r	s	t	a	b	m	t	y	x
G	k	x	y	z	t	z	b	a	o	p	q	y	z	t	m	n	e	f	g	r	a	b	h	i	j	x	v
H	t	m	p	o	q	r	s	x	c	d	f	b	c	d	m	t	o	a	c	d	e	a	c	e	d	e	x
I	g	h	i	x	y	m	a	b	o	o	p	q	o	m	p	z	r	s	t	y	t	z	v	v	w	x	b
J	w	x	y	t	z	a	p	q	r	x	t	z	o	z	o	b	c	d	o	t	m	c	a	f	g	h	c
K	x	m	z	o	a	b	f	h	z	v	n	o	a	z	j	i	n	t	x	y	p	r	s	t	z	n	x
L	y	o	g	h	i	v	z	t	m	n	o	i	i	p	a	r	s	t	a	t	o	m	x	y	z	a	b
M	m	c	d	e	t	z	v	a	h	i	j	v	t	x	m	n	o	x	t	a	b	c	v	d	e	f	x
N	p	q	r	a	b	n	z	t	o	k	l	m	p	q	r	x	y	t	a	b	z	c	d	e	y	x	o
O	v	x	y	t	z	b	o	m	n	a	v	y	t	e	f	g	l	m	n	x	a	j	k	l	t	z	p

2 Hold a pencil by its unsharpened end at arm's length with your arm stretched stiffly in front of you.

Draw a continuous line over all the Xs and under all the Os in each line.

a	x x x x x o o o o o o x x x x x o o o o o o
b	x o o o o o o x x x x x x x x o o o o o o
c	x x o o o o o o x x x x x x x o o o o o o x
d	x x x o o o o o o o x x x x x x x o o o o o o x
e	x x x x o o o o o o o x x x x o o o o o o o x x
f	o o o o o o x x x x x x x x o o o o o o o x x

Values: A Programme for Primary Schools ISBN 978-1845900823

Doing Your Best

All these people want to do better. Write what advice you would give each one. Don't just state what they should do, give sound advice on how to do it.

I did badly in the spelling test again and my stories are marked down because of my poor spelling.

I want to become the shooter for our school netball team, but lately I keep missing easy shots.

I want to be the fastest runner in my year, but I seem to get puffed out too quickly.

When I leave school I want to have a job in which I can serve and help others less fortunate.

Cooperation

Introduction

COOPERATION – being able to work or act happily together with other people.

- Have students use their dictionaries to find and write the definition of **cooperation**.

- Students describe the different ways they can cooperate by completing these sentences.

  I can cooperate at school by ______________
  I can cooperate at home by ______________
  I can cooperate on the school bus by ______________

- Explain to students that cooperation is not necessarily doing something active. It may be just sitting and listening for a given time.

- Ask students to give examples of active cooperation and passive cooperation.

  Examples
  - I want everyone to walk over to that pole
  - I want everyone to watch how I do this sum.

- Provide students with lots of group activities and games that rely on cooperation for a successful conclusion.

- Students form small teams and must cooperate to make the longest lists in given categories in three minutes, e.g. names of birds, body parts, things that have wheels, things that are round, fruits and vegetables, three or four letter words.

Cooperation

1 Cooperative Picture

For this activity you must work in groups of three. The idea is for your group to create the best car together.

One member must draw the front of the car, another draws the middle and the other draws the rear. When completed, display your group's car and share your picture with the other groups.

Rear	Middle	Front

2 Team Treasure Hunt

This game can be played in small groups but it needs cooperation from each member for a group to be successful. The idea is for your team to be the first to collect all the items below by searching in the playground.

a bottle top	lollipop stick	a feather	a smooth stone
a blade of green grass	a blade of dry grass	a snail shell	
a coloured petal	a lolly wrapper	a rough stone	a round leaf

Values: A Programme for Primary Schools ISBN 978-184590082-3

Cooperation

1 These are some jobs to be done at home. Add three more. Tick the correct columns. Compare your chart with those of your friends.

Work/Activity	Parents Only	Children Only	Either
cooking meals			
washing the family car			
ironing			
cleaning rooms			
doing dishes			
shopping			
feeding pets			

2 Work in groups of 4. Your class is going to the zoo. You are only allowed to take 5 of these things. Your group must choose which ones. Check your choices with those made by other groups.

spending money sunglasses notebook and pencils
mobile phone suncream comics to read on the bus
camera bottle of squash computer game hat

Humour

Introduction

HUMOUR – being able to perceive and express what is amusing or comical.

- Discuss with students the kinds of things that make them laugh. Let them brainstorm the funniest jokes they have heard or things they have seen.

- Ask students to consider the differences between laughing at something that is truly funny or finding amusement in something that may be hurtful.

- Should you find these things amusing?
  - Lynda is running across the yard and trips over, injuring her ankle.
  - Patrick's mother cannot afford for him to have his hair cut at a hairdresser's. Instead she cuts it herself as best she can. Sometimes it is uneven.
  - Toni is a new class member recently arrived from America. Some of your classmates call her a yank.

- Have students discuss situations that some may laugh at, but which can be hurtful and cruel.

- Write the following proverb on the board and have students discuss its meaning.

He who laughs last laughs best.

- Students make up stories or plays in which someone had the first laugh against another, but that person was able to laugh last.

- Ask students to tell the class their favourite joke. Have a "Laugh in Class!" day.

Humour

HAVE A LAUGH IN CLASS

1 a Read this joke.

After lunch one day a boy returned late for class.
"Why are you late?" demanded the teacher.
"I'm late, Sir, because I was throwing peanuts in the river!" replied the boy.
"Get to your seat!" growled the teacher.
A few minutes later another boy arrived.
"And why are you late for class?" yelled the enraged teacher.
"I'm late Sir because I was throwing peanuts in the river."
"Get to your seat immediately!" demanded the teacher.
Shortly after, another boy, whose hair and clothes were dripping wet entered the classroom. "And why are you so late?" growled the frustrated teacher.
"I'm Peanuts," replied the boy.

b Draw the joke as a comic strip in the boxes below.
Use speech balloons to show what people are saying.

2 Play this giggle game.

Players line up opposite each other in two teams of six, eight or ten. Team 1 tries to make all the players in Team 2 smile or laugh. As each player laughs or smiles they are out and must leave their place. The team that gets all the other players out in the shortest time is the winner.

Humour

HAVE A LAUGH IN CLASS

1 Read the following jokes.

Q. Why did the monster paint himself in rainbow-coloured stripes?
A. He wanted to hide in the crayon box.

Knock Knock
Who's there?
Arthur
Arthur who?
Arthur any more at home like you?

Q. What's brown and sticky?
A. A stick.

Q. Where do polar bears vote?
A. The North Poll.

Q. Why did the tomato turn red?
A. It saw the salad dressing!

Which joke do you like best? Explain why you think the one you chose is funnier than the others.

____

____

2 Silly Questions

A man is sitting at the end of the pier holding his fishing rod with his line dangling in the water, when someone comes past and says, "Are you fishing?"
"No. I'm just drowning worms!" replied the man.

In pairs make up your own situation in which someone asks a silly question and you give a funny reply.

Values: A Programme for Primary Schools ISBN 978-184590082-3 © 2008 Blake Education and Crown House Publishing

Generosity

Introduction

GENEROSITY – unselfish and always ready to give and to share with others.

- Ask students to explain what they think is meant by the word **generosity**.

  Have them relate stories of a person being generous.
- Conduct a class debate on the topic, "Should everyone in our country have to give part of their income to help people in poorer countries?"
- Students discuss whether it is fair for some people in the community to have lots of money while some have very little.
- Students to brainstorm ways a person can be generous without giving away money.
- Students discuss the difference between these two sentences.
  - Mary has done well with the money she won.
  - Mary has done good with the money she won.
- Students create short plays in which someone's generosity helps another.
- Students to write humorous stories that are linked to well known fairytales. e.g. What if Cinderella's sisters had been generous rather than mean?

Generosity

Are you a generous person? Are you always prepared to help others?

Complete the following sentences in your own words. Think carefully before you answer each one.

1 When someone is nice to me I ______________________________

____

2 The one thing I really like doing is ______________________________

____

3 The thing I am most concerned about is ______________________________

____

4 When someone helps me I ______________________________

____

5 I really enjoy it when ______________________________

____

6 I like my classmates because ______________________________

____

7 If I was Prime Minister, the first thing I would do is ______________________________

____

8 I am happiest when ______________________________

____

9 I always feel sad when ______________________________

____

10 Something I do to help my classmates is ______________________________

____

11 Something I do to help my parents is ______________________________

____

12 Others like it when I ______________________________

____

Generosity

Imagine the following was said to you.
Write replies in the balloon that show you are not only caring but also generous.

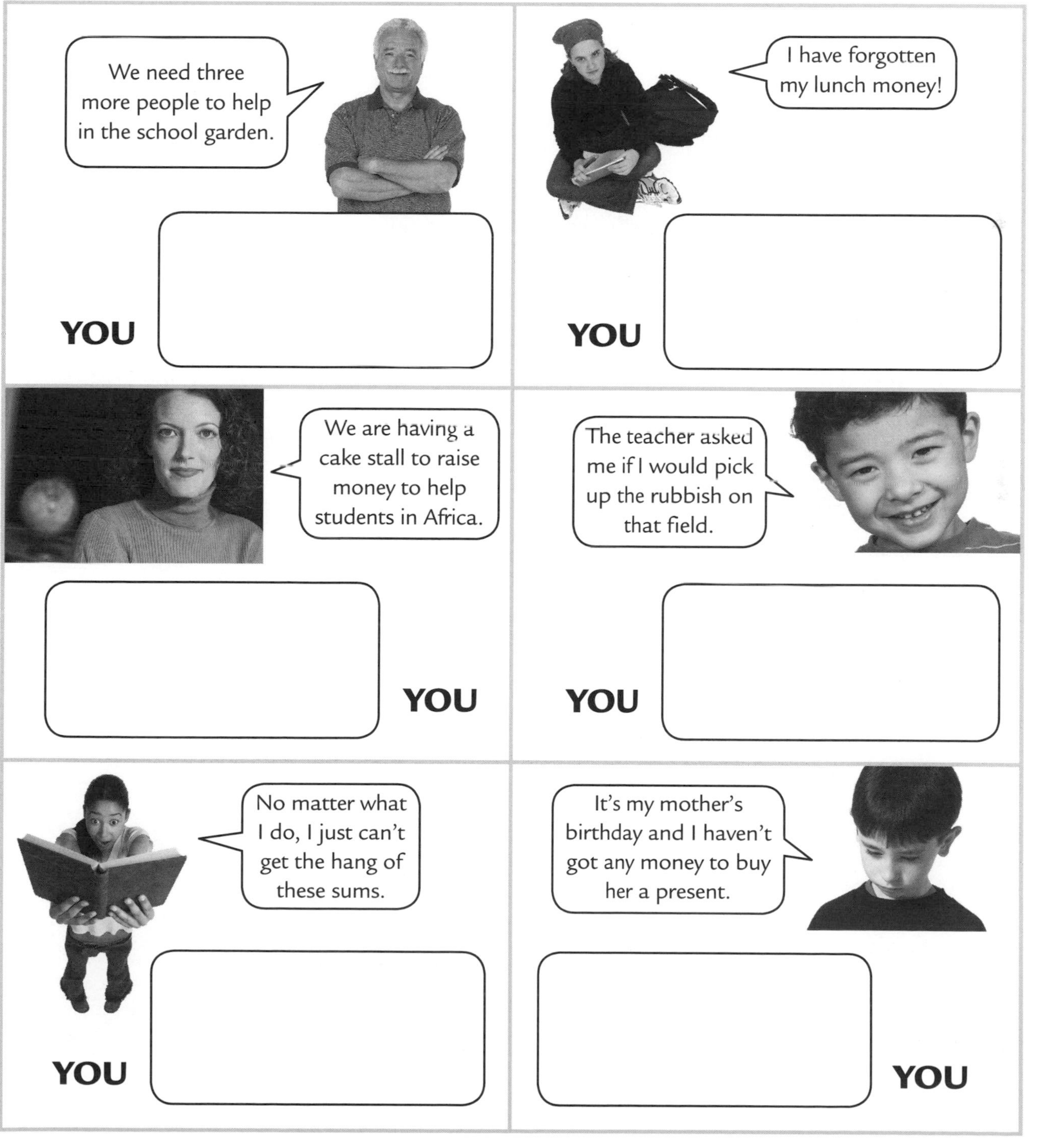

Values: A Programme for Primary Schools ISBN 978-184590082-3

Creativity

Introduction

CREATIVITY – the ability to think and create in an original way.

- Discuss with students what is meant by the term **creativity**. Ask them to tell you in what subjects they are most creative, e.g. art, craft.
- Provide each pupil with a piece of A4 paper. Challenge them to use it to create something that is useful.
- Students form small groups and brainstorm the many inventions that make their lives easier. All of these inventions are the result of someone or some group of people being creative.
- Encourage students to create some novel excuses.

  Examples
  - I'm sorry I'm late for school but the train had a flat tyre.
  - I'm sorry about my homework sheet but I turned it into a paper aeroplane and someone hijacked it.

Students can write these on a large sheet of paper to be displayed in the classroom.

- Choose different objects and challenge students to write one similarity and one difference between them.

  Examples
  - a duck and a guinea pig
  - a leopard and a flea
  - a table and a flower

Creativity

How creative are you? Test yourself by completing the activities on this page.

1 Write down at least 5 uses for a piece of used chewing gum. Draw one of them.

2 Using a pen, draw an everyday object from each of these circles, e.g. a clock.

3 Design a kitchen utensil that would be useful for peeling grapes. Describe how it works.

4 Make up sentences by using each letter of one word to make another word. e.g **MEAT** could be **M**ice **E**at **A**nd **T**alk.

Creativity

How creative are you? Test yourself by completing each of these sentence starters.

1 What if	**2** How come
3 Why did	**4** How many times
5 Why is it	**6** Where would
7 How many ways	**8** Why didn't

Assertiveness

Introduction

ASSERTIVENESS – being prepared to take a stand on things you strongly believe in.

- Ask students to suggest what they think **assertiveness** means. Encourage them to discuss when it pays to be assertive.
- Students brainstorm the ways they can look and act confidently.

  Examples
  - speak clearly
  - don't smile too much in a nervous way
  - look into other people's eyes and not at the ground
- Discuss how children can deal with bullies. In small groups, they brainstorm the ways they can prevent themselves or others from being bullied.

  Example
  - Ask students how they can assert themselves over would-be bullies.
  - Discuss what is meant by the saying:

Those who don't stand for something will fall for anything.

- Students develop colourful posters stating ways they can stand up for themselves.

  Example

  Stand tall.

  Stay in control of yourself.

Assertiveness

How assertive are you?

1 If the teacher says something which I know is wrong, I will tell them.
☐ always ☐ sometimes ☐ never

2 If a bigger pupil pushes me out of the lunch queue, I stand up for myself.
☐ always ☐ sometimes ☐ never

3 If the teacher blames me for something I didn't do, I will defend myself.
☐ always ☐ sometimes ☐ never

4 When a bigger pupil deliberately knocks me over, I demand he or she apologise.
☐ always ☐ sometimes ☐ never

5 If classmates tell me I cannot play with their group, I demand to be able to and push in.
☐ always ☐ sometimes ☐ never

6 If a classmate asks me to do something wrong, like stealing money, I say no.
☐ always ☐ sometimes ☐ never

7 If I see a pupil do something wrong in the playground, I immediately tell them not to do it again.
☐ always ☐ sometimes ☐ never

8 If I am not as good as others at something, I practise hard to get better.
☐ always ☐ sometimes ☐ never

9 If I have to give a report or speech to the whole class or school, I feel happy and relaxed.
☐ always ☐ sometimes ☐ never

10 If my teacher does not give me something or discriminates against me, I report them to the head.
☐ always ☐ sometimes ☐ never

11 If my older brother or sister takes something that belongs to me, I make them give it back.
☐ always ☐ sometimes ☐ never

12 When I meet a group of students for the first time, I feel shy and timid.
☐ always ☐ sometimes ☐ never

Score always = 3 sometimes = 2 never = 1 My score is ____________

If you scored 25 or more you are quite assertive.

- Discuss your answers with your classmates.
- Discuss if there are times when people can be too assertive.

Assertiveness

This is a conversation you hear one day in the playground.

Two boys are arguing over who owns a computer game. Both are trying to assert their ownership. Later, one of the teachers asks you what happened. Write what is said.

1 Fill in the missing words in the conversation.

Mike Give it to ______________ . It is ____________________

Jack No ______________ . It is ____________________

Mike It's ______________ I'll tell ____________________

Jack Of ______________ it's mine. Isn't it Mandy?

Mandy Yes Mike, it is ______________

Susan Nah. Mandy you're ______________ . It is Mike's. I saw him bring it to ______________ yesterday.

Mike See I told you ______________ .

Jack Who would ever ______________ Susan. She always sucks up to Mike.

Mike Well I'd ______________ Susan before __________ because she is a dork.

Jack Come on Mike ______________ it back to me.

Mike Go jump in the ______________ you loser.

Jack I ______________ it, now give it to __________________ .

Mike If you ______________ me again I'll hit you.

Jack I didn't ______________ you. Now let go of my __________________ .

Mike Stop it!

Jack Not ______________ I've got it back.

Mike Ouch! You ______________ then cop __________________ .

Jack Oooh! You ______________ that was hard. Well cop __________________

2 Your report for the teacher.

____

____

____

____

____

Patience

■ Introduction

PATIENCE – being calm when waiting.

- Write the word **patience** on the board. Have students suggest what it means.
- Discuss the possible reasons for some people being more patient than others.
- What type of things test your patience? e.g. A younger sister who touches your things? Students brainstorm these things and share them with each other.
- Students to name people they know who are very patient. In what ways do they show patience?
- Students describe what it is like trying to please someone who is impatient.
- On a sheet of paper have students draw a path divided into stepping stones. This will become their "Pathway of Patience". In each block students write when you need to have patience.

THE PATHWAY OF PATIENCE

e.g.

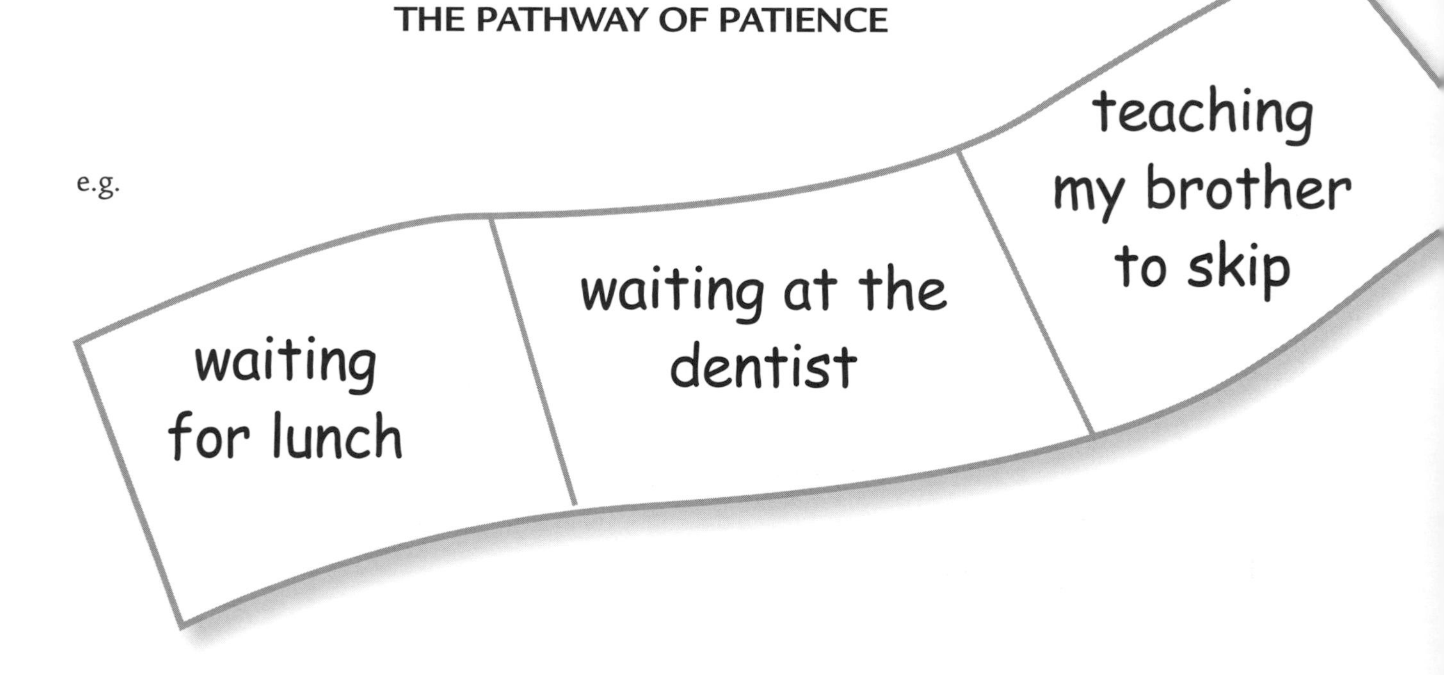

Patience

1 Are you a patient person? Do you get upset when others are taking a long time to do something?

a If you put your hand up and the teacher has not noticed, do you cough loudly or begin yelling out?

☐ always ☐ sometimes ☐ never

b If something of yours does not work, do you toss it in the bin straight way?

☐ always ☐ sometimes ☐ never

c If you are waiting to go outside and your brother is taking a long time to get his shoes on, do you yell at him to hurry up?

☐ always ☐ sometimes ☐ never

d If you are getting on a bus and the other people are taking their time, do you get angry?

☐ always ☐ sometimes ☐ never

e If your parents are taking you to a party and they are late getting to the car, do you yell at them to hurry?

☐ always ☐ sometimes ☐ never

f If there is a long queue at the canteen, do you push a smaller pupil out of the line and take their place?

☐ always ☐ sometimes ☐ never

g When you are waiting for an adult to serve you a meal, do you get angry if you have to wait a long time?

☐ always ☐ sometimes ☐ never

h When you are waiting for your birthday or Christmas to come, do you become impatient?

☐ always ☐ sometimes ☐ never

i Do you get upset when your parents are watching their favourite show and you can't turn to your favourite show?

☐ always ☐ sometimes ☐ never

j Do you get angry when you ask someone something and they take a long time to make up their minds?

☐ always ☐ sometimes ☐ never

2 Have you ever been angry at having to wait? Write about it.

____

____

3 Do you get impatient waiting to grow up, or do you hope time moves slowly? Give a reason for your answer.

____

Patience

What would you say to the following people?

Tolerance

Introduction

TOLERANCE – being able to accept the differences and opinions of others without bigotry.

- Discuss with students what the word **tolerance** means. Question why they believe some people are intolerant of others.

  Examples
  - Do you get angry if your younger brother takes a long time to get his shoes on?
  - Do you get angry with people in the street who ask others for money?

- Students brainstorm the reasons why people may be intolerant of others, e.g. different physical features, different skin colour, different interests, different customs and traditions.
- Discuss what these intolerances lead to, e.g. racial discrimination.
- If you have been refused a job because you are too tall, you have experienced discrimination. Ask students to explain why sometimes people discriminate against others.
- Ask students if they know what the word stereotyping means. Discuss why certain people become stereotyped. e.g. Billy's father is in prison for stealing so Billy is sure to steal too.
- Have students give examples of any kinds of stereotyping they know.
- Ask them to talk about the types of people who often suffer from being stereotyped.

Tolerance

This is a group activity in which all members of the group must work together to achieve the task.

There are no right or wrong answers and each group may have completely different answers. This does not matter. However it is important that your group works together so that all member contributions are accepted seriously. The final list must be agreed on by all members.

Task Your friends are going fishing. You will be camping out on the river bank for three nights. Here is a list of twenty things your group is able to take with them. Your task is to list the twenty items in order from most important to least important. Write 1 as the *most* important and 20 as the *least* important.

- ☐ comics
- ☐ insect repellant
- ☐ knife
- ☐ fishing lines
- ☐ kettle
- ☐ tent
- ☐ saucepan
- ☐ sleeping bags
- ☐ fishing bait
- ☐ canned food
- ☐ wide-brimmed hats
- ☐ teddy bear
- ☐ raincoats
- ☐ torches
- ☐ radio
- ☐ first-aid kit
- ☐ frying pan
- ☐ mobile telephone
- ☐ milk
- ☐ lighter or matches

Values: A Programme for Primary Schools ISBN 978-184590082-3

Tolerance

Explain what you would do each time.

1 Bronson borrowed your cricket bat last week. Each day you ask for it back, but he tells you he has forgotten it again.	**2** Terina accidentally spills some muddy water over your project book.
3 Lucas told you he wants you to come and stay for the weekend, but he keeps putting it off.	**4** Tai often calls you nasty names because you have dark skin.
5 James borrowed your bicycle and got a puncture in both tyres. He told you he would fix them as soon as he gets the time. It's been a month and they are still not repaired.	**6** Michelle plays netball for your team. Michelle can't play very well and you have lost games because of this. You know she has her heart set on playing each time.

Values: A Programme for Primary Schools ISBN 978-1845900823

Forgiveness

Introduction

FORGIVENESS – ceasing to have bad feelings against another for what they may have done to you.

- Discuss with students what is meant by the word **forgiveness**. When do you forgive someone?
- Students name people in legends and stories who were prepared to forgive. e.g. Cinderella forgave the Ugly Sisters.
- Write the following saying on the board.

Love your enemies. It will drive them crazy.

- Discuss what this means.
- Ask students to share their experiences of forgiving someone or being forgiven by someone.
- Ask students to think about the following question.

Is it easier to forgive someone who accidentally hurt you than it is to forgive someone who harmed you deliberately? Why?

Students share their thoughts.

- Students discuss this saying.

If revenge is sweet why does it leave such a bitter taste?

Forgiveness

1a If someone deliberately hits you, you will hit them back.

☐ always ☐ sometimes ☐ never

b When someone does something wrong, you get your own back by spreading gossip about them.

☐ always ☐ sometimes ☐ never

c If you know a classmate has stolen something from you, you would steal something of theirs.

☐ always ☐ sometimes ☐ never

d If your parents won't let you stay at a friend's place, you sulk.

☐ always ☐ sometimes ☐ never

e If someone harmed your younger brother or sister, you would get revenge in some way.

☐ always ☐ sometimes ☐ never

f If your parents won't buy you something you want, you get your own back by breaking something or not doing your chores.

☐ always ☐ sometimes ☐ never

g When a classmate tells the teacher about something naughty you did, you try to get back at him or her.

☐ always ☐ sometimes ☐ never

h If you learn that a classmate is making up lies about you, you make up lies about them.

☐ always ☐ sometimes ☐ never

i If someone bumped into you accidentally, you would punch them or hurt them in some way.

☐ always ☐ sometimes ☐ never

j A classmate trips over and skins their knees and arms. You don't like them so you encourage the other students to laugh.

☐ always ☐ sometimes ☐ never

2 Some people claim that revenge against someone who has harmed you is part of the "healing process". Do you agree or disagree? Give reasons.

____

____

3 Do you forgive someone easily or do you hold grudges? Think about it.

4 **To err is human, to forgive divine.**

Do you know what this saying means? Discuss it with your classmates.

Forgiveness

1 Decorate this saying.

People with clenched fists cannot shake hands.

2 In the squares below draw a comic strip. Tim does something wrong. It makes John very angry. Eventually John is able to forgive Tim.

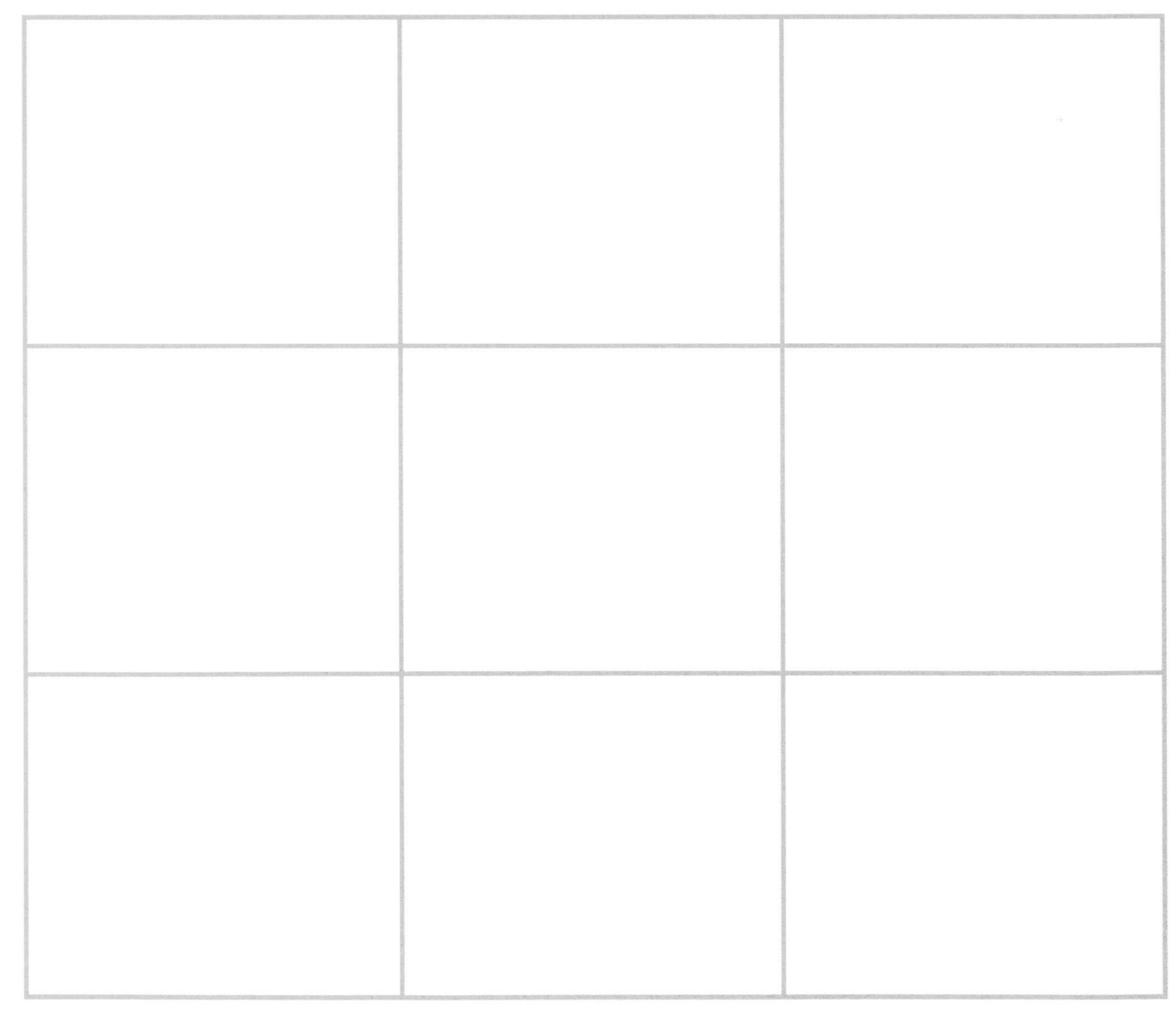

Values: A Programme for Primary Schools ISBN 978-184590082-3

Enthusiasm

Introduction

*ENTHUSIASM – **having a strong and eager interest in a particular area.***

- Introduce the word **enthusiasm** to students. Have them suggest what it means.
- Students name those things they are most enthusiastic about. Why are you more enthusiastic about one thing than another?

- Ask students to discuss what this means. Ask them if they ever get bored. Why?
- Students form small groups and brainstorm the things they like to do and are enthusiastic about, and the things they don't like to do. Ask them to explain when they are not enthusiastic.
- A person is bored with school. What are some things we could do to make them more enthusiastic? Have students share their thoughts.
- Design a brightly coloured poster that will help students become enthusiastic about using the school library.

Enthusiasm

Read the story then complete the activities.

Galloping gumboots – from farming to fame

Cliff Young, ignoring the ever-increasing importance of scientific training techniques in athletics, recorded one of the most incredible victories in Australian sporting history, using his own primitive and unorthodox methods. If a film scriptwriter suggested a story about a potato farmer who took up running when nearly sixty and won one of the world's greatest endurance tests, smashing the race record by nearly two days, a producer could easily reject it as too fanciful. Yet in May 1983, Cliff Young became a national folk hero doing just that, winning the 875 kilometre Sydney-to-Melbourne race.

Cliff, by far the oldest competitor at sixty-one, blitzed his younger rivals to complete the course in five days and fifteen hours, sleeping just eleven hours along the way. He had taken up running only three years before, after an unsuccessful hang-gliding attempt, because he wanted to achieve something before he died. His preparation included galloping in gumboots around his potato patch, chasing cows and eating such food mixtures as tinned peas with pumpkin. However, the modest, unassuming runner had something else going for him – enthusiasm, courage and a relentless determination. Young needed it in large doses, for he had extra obstacles to contend with. For one thing, he ran in ventilated, long plastic pants to shield skin cancers on his legs. For another, he had dislocated his shoulder. When approached with medication, he shrugged it off saying, "I'm not letting nobody stick no needles in me." Despite the difficulties, this marvellous marathon machine not only won, but slashed one day and nineteen hours off the course record. It is little wonder that his incredible effort captured the imagination of the Australian public; many people find it tiring enough just driving that distance. Typical of the man was the generous gesture with one thousand of the ten thousand dollars in prize money: "I'm going to give something to all those who finished."

From *Make Your Own Rainbow* – Leonard Ryzman

1 What was Cliff Young's occupation?

____

2 Why did Cliff take up running?

____

____

3 What were some of the difficulties Cliff overcame?

____

____

4 How do we know Cliff was not only enthusiastic, but also very generous?

____

____

Values: A Programme for Primary Schools ISBN 978-1845900823 © 2008 Blake Education and Crown House Publishing

Enthusiasm

Being enthusiastic improves our chances of being successful. It also makes us more popular with classmates who know we are really trying to achieve something.

How could you display your enthusiasm in each of these circumstances? Remember it is not always pleasant to be enthusiastic in some situations but you must try.

1 Lockie and you are playing in a doubles tennis match tomorrow. It is the grand final.	**2** Your mother tells you your cousins are visiting next weekend. You don't like them very much.
3 The teacher wants to organise a concert for the end of the school year. You will be expected to perform an item.	**4** Eve wants you to come camping next weekend.
5 You are playing football. Your team is ten goals behind at half time.	**6** Your parents want you to learn the piano but you hate piano lessons. Tomorrow there is a concert and your parents are coming to hear you play.

Values: A Programme for Primary Schools ISBN 978-184590082-3

Independence

Introduction

INDEPENDENCE – having the ability to act and work alone without the need of help from others.

- Discuss with students what they think **independence** means.
- Many countries of the world celebrate their own Independence Day, e.g. the United States of America. Ask students to discuss what this means.
- Have students role-play stories in which the teacher leaves the room and some students misbehave. Have them suggest the consequences of such behaviour.
- A teacher once said:

**"I'll treat you like adults if you act like adults.
I'll treat you like children if you act like children."**

Students share their ideas about what they think the teacher meant.

- Some people in Australia want to change their form of government to a republic. Conduct a class debate on this.
- Students make a list of things they are already showing independence in, e.g. tidying their room, catching the bus to school, looking after pets.
- Ask them to list things they are still dependent on, e.g. pocket money from their parents.
- Ask students to list the following under the correct heading.

water	**pocket money**	**bike**	**food**	**clothing**
horse	**books**	**toys**	**home**	**video games**

Needs **Wants** **Luxuries**

Independence

Think about how independent you are. Do your parents still have to make your bed? Do you earn your pocket money?

Below is a grid numbered 1 to 12. On the left-hand side, write down 12 things you like to do (the order does not matter), e.g. watch television, do homework, go to a party.

- Write the date you last did it.
- Write **self** if you enjoy doing it by yourself or write **others** if you enjoy it more when you are doing it with others.
- Add a star if you need help from your parents to do it.
- In the final column write a **C** if you need help from classmates or friends to do it.

Activity	Date	Self/Others	*	C
1				
2				
3				
4				
5				
6				
7				
8				
9				
10				
11				
12				

Independence

My Personal Timeline

A personal timeline highlights experiences that make up your life.
On the lines below list significant events that have influenced or affected your life.

Include such things as:

- learning to crawl
- birthdays
- losing your first tooth
- operations/illnesses
- special celebrations
- sport/other achievements
- your first tooth
- birth of your brothers or sisters
- riding a bike
- holidays
- clubs/cubs, scouts, brownies etc.
- beginning school

Values: A Programme for Primary Schools ISBN 978-184590082-3

Flexibility

Introduction

FLEXIBILITY – having the ability to change or adapt to new things.

- Have students suggest what they think **flexibility** means. What do we mean when we say a piece of metal is flexible? Students share their answers.

> **Japanese proverb**
> **The bamboo that bends is stronger than the oak that resists.**

- Discuss what this saying means.
- Students discuss mythical characters who change quickly, e.g. Superman, Batman. What special powers do these people possess that make them so flexible?
- Ask students to share their experiences about having to change. How do they feel when they have to change?

  Example ◆ My best friend at school was Shaun, but then he left to live overseas. We did lots together. I felt sad and empty the day he left.

- Someone says, "Get over it".
  Are some things harder to get over than others? Students discuss.

Flexibility

It is important that throughout our lives we are flexible and able to accept change. The things we liked when we were young are not always the same ones we like today.

1 Read the activities below. Tick the correct columns for you.

Activity	When I began school		Today	
	Liked	**Did not like**	**Like**	**Do not like**
a playing games				
b eating carrots				
c helping wash dishes				
d reading books				
e drawing				
f watching television				
g loud music				
h playing on a team				
i going on a school trip				
j skipping				
k eating sweet things				
l eating fruit				
m staying overnight at a friend's house				
n staying with my grandparents				
o physical education lessons				
p going to the dentist				

2 Have you changed much? How?

____

____

3 Do you like more or less things now?

____

____

Flexibility

How well do you accept change? The following is a test to measure how quickly you can adapt to changes.

1 Below are 24 common five-letter words with their letters jumbled. See how long it takes you to write each one correctly. You must begin at **a** and work in alphabetical order.

a bursh ____________
b ssorc ____________
c hsams ____________
d tfihs ____________
e hserf ____________
f htlif ____________
g lemac ____________
h ytrap ____________
i throf ____________
j tshix ____________
k tolch ____________
l raftd ____________
m rgpsa ____________
n marts ____________
o skrpa ____________
p wlris ____________
q netre ____________
r tnrub ____________
s trups ____________
t ratni ____________
u garny ____________
v ayspn ____________
w eahts ____________
x zeabl ____________

2 Some words in this story have their first and last letters in their correct order but the ones in the middle are jumbled. Can you read the story without pausing?

One fine snnuy day a man found a ptsailc bucket on the side of the road. He filled the bucket with wtear and crriead it to his home at the bttoom of the muontian. Each day he used the bckuet to water his vgeabltee patch. He grew ctrraos, baens and lcttuces.

Values: A Programme for Primary Schools ISBN 978-1845900823

Thoughtfulness

Introduction

THOUGHTFULNESS – being at all times considerate and kind to others.

- Discuss with students what they think is meant by **thoughtfulness**.
- The suffix **ful** means "full of" so thoughtfulness means **"full of thought"**.
- Ask students what these words mean.

  beautiful **plentiful** **hopeful** **careful**

- Students discuss the differences in meaning between:

  I think of you a lot.

  I think a lot of you.

- Students share their experiences of when someone has been thoughtful towards them, e.g. visited them when they were ill, offered them a loan of their pen, listened carefully to their worries.
- Students make a thoughtfulness chart to display in the classroom. On it they record all the ways they have been thoughtful to others.

Our thoughtful chart
On Friday we cleaned up the store room.
Last week we picked up litters in the playground.

Thoughtfulness

How thoughtful are you? Do you think about the feelings of others? Circle your choices.

1 **Laughing** is fun but sometimes laughing can be thoughtless or even cruel. When is it fun to laugh?

- when someone tells a funny joke
- when you see someone fall down
- watching a comedy on television
- when someone does something that looks funny but is very embarrassing to them

2 **Running** at school is sometimes silly because you or another person can get hurt. When is it right to run at school?

- during a fire drill
- when you do an errand for your teacher
- when you play games on the oval
- when you are doing physical education

5 **Asking** for help is important at school. When is the best time to ask your teacher for help?

- when your teacher is not busy
- during a maths or spelling test
- when your teacher is talking to the head teacher
- when your teacher is helping your group

6 **Telling** teachers things is sometimes important as long as it is not 'telling tales'. When should you tell a teacher something?

- when you see someone writing on the school walls
- when someone cuts in front of you in line
- when a bully is threatening a younger pupil
- when someone calls you a bad name

7 **Asking** questions is something we all do. We must remember to ask questions for the correct purpose. When and what questions should you ask?.

- when you want to find out a secret about people so you can poke fun at them
- when you want some information so you will be able to help another person
- to help you learn about someone so you understand their problems better
- to find out things you can gossip about

Thoughtfulness

In the following situations describe how you can show others you are thoughtful. What are some practical things you could do to help?

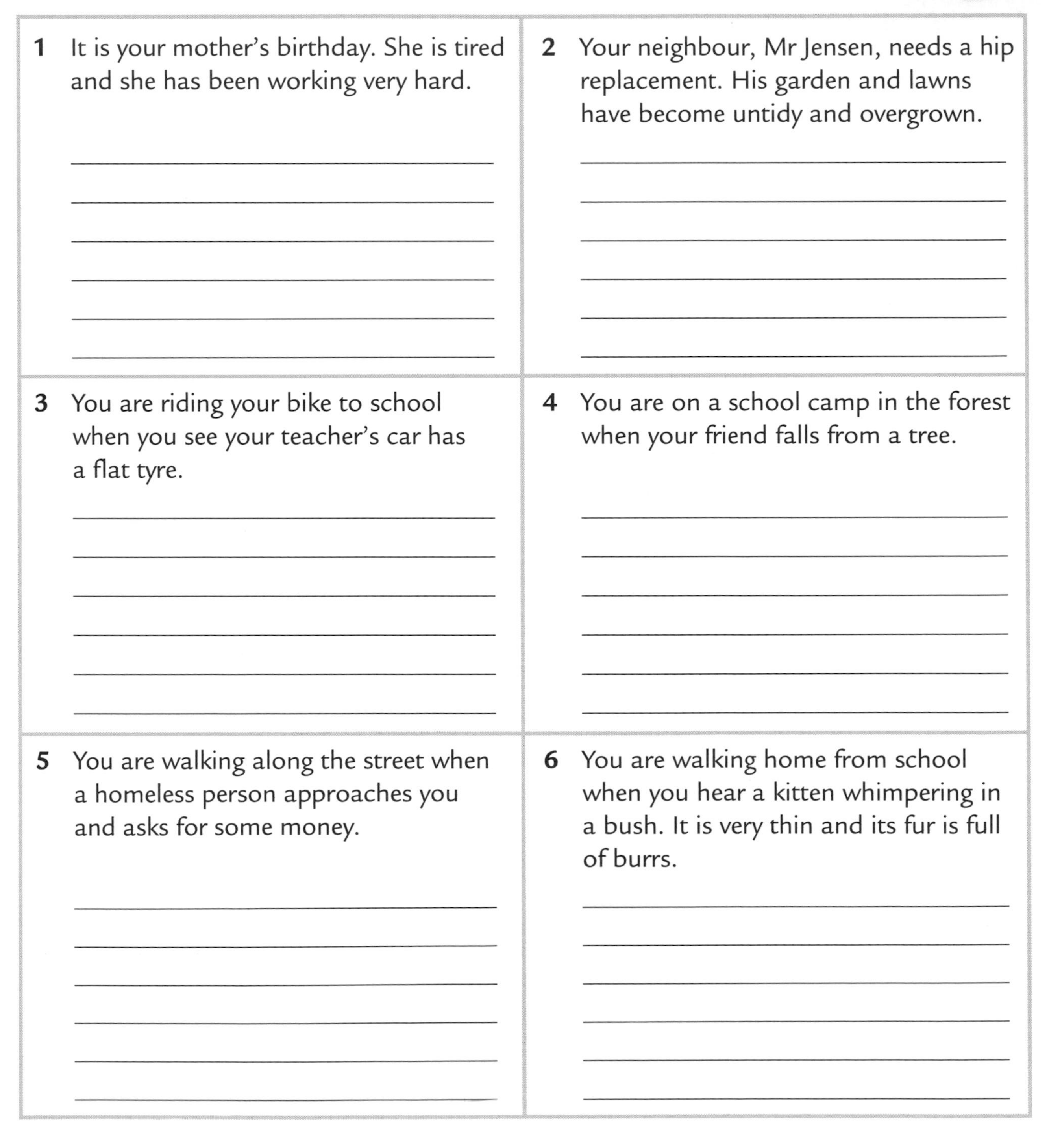

1 It is your mother's birthday. She is tired and she has been working very hard.

2 Your neighbour, Mr Jensen, needs a hip replacement. His garden and lawns have become untidy and overgrown.

3 You are riding your bike to school when you see your teacher's car has a flat tyre.

4 You are on a school camp in the forest when your friend falls from a tree.

5 You are walking along the street when a homeless person approaches you and asks for some money.

6 You are walking home from school when you hear a kitten whimpering in a bush. It is very thin and its fur is full of burrs.

Values: A Programme for Primary Schools ISBN 978-184590082-3 © 2008 Blake Education and Crown House Publishing

Perseverance

Introduction

PERSEVERANCE – having the ability to continue to maintain a purpose in spite of difficulties.

- Have students discuss what they think **perseverance** means.
- Tell the students the following story from *Make Your Own Rainbow* by Leonard Ryzman.

  When Roy Thackerson was six years old, he played with a stick of dynamite which blew the fingers off his left hand, and claimed his left eye. He came to be regarded as one of the best country and western fiddlers in the United States, and he also plays guitar. He has stubs left of his fingers, yet moves them with an amazing dexterity that I had to see to believe. You would not have thought it possible. But the feeling that he could still play music was so strong, he would not let go of his dream.
- Ask students to share stories about people who kept persevering under difficulties.
- Students write the following saying on a sheet of A4 paper. Ask them to illustrate it.

  A quitter never wins; a winner never quits.
- Students write stories about famous people who persevered and finally achieved success.
- Ask students to describe what the world would be like:
  - if the Wright brothers didn't persevere in trying to fly.
  - if Captain Cook didn't persevere in trying to discover Australia.
  - if Thomas Edison didn't persevere with inventing a reliable electric light.

Perseverance

Bruce and the Spider **by Eliza Cook**

King Bruce of Scotland flung himself down, in a lonely mood, to think;
True he was a monarch, and wore a crown, but his heart was beginning to sink.
For he had been trying to do a great deed, to make his people glad;

He had tried and tried, but couldn't succeed, and so he became quite sad.
He flung himself down in a low despair, as grieved as man could be;
And after a while, as he pondered there, "I'll give it all up," said he.
Now, just at the moment, a spider dropped, with its silken cobweb clew;
And the king, in the midst of his thinking, stopped to see what the spider would do.

'Twas a long way up to the ceiling dome, and it hung by a rope so fine
That, how it would get to its cobweb home, King Bruce could not divine.
It soon began to cling and crawl straight up with strong endeavour;
But down it came, with a slipping sprawl, as near to the ground as ever.

Up, up, it ran, not a second did stay to utter the least complaint,
Till it fell still lower; and there it lay, a little dizzy and faint.
Its head grew steady—again it went, and travelled a half-yard higher;
'Twas a delicate thread it had to tread, and a road where its feet would tire.

Again it fell, and swung below; but up it quickly mounted,
Till up and down, now fast, now slow, nine brave attempts were counted.
"Sure," cried the king, "that foolish thing will strive no more to climb,
When it toils so hard to reach and cling, and tumbles every time.

But up the spider went once more; ah me! 'tis an anxious minute;
It's only a foot from the cobweb door; oh, say, will he lose or win it?
Steadily, steadily, inch by inch, higher and higher he got;
And a bold little run at the very last pinch put him into the wished-for spot.

"Bravo! Bravo!" the king cried out. "All honour to those who try;
The spider up there defied despair. He conquered, and why shouldn't I?"
And Bruce of Scotland braced his mind, and gossips tell the tale
That he tried once more as he tried before, and that time he did not fail.

Pay goodly heed, all you who read, and beware of saying "I can't;"
'Tis a cowardly word, and apt to lead to idleness, folly, and want.

This poem tells how a spider showed a man that if you persevere you will eventually achieve what you want. Robert Bruce was defeated by an English army and went into hiding, but he continued to persevere and finally defeated the English in a battle at Bannockburn in 1314.

Perseverance

Read the passage then complete the activities below.

Along the rocky road from rags to riches

Some years ago, I was walking along a street in New York, unaware that an unemployed young man walking nearby with less than one hundred dollars to his name was about to experience three days which would ultimately have an impact on film theatres even thousands of miles away. Some time later, in Los Angeles, a friend, Gerry, urged me to see a film which he insisted would win the Academy Award for Best Picture. I thought Gerry was being overly optimistic. After all, at that stage, I had never heard of the writer-director-actor around whom it revolved.

Sylvester Stallone was born in New York. While trying to become a star, he cleaned out lions' cages at Central Park Zoo, where one lion with an urgent call of nature, spoilt Stallone's only pair of trousers. He cleaned fish, worked as a cinema usher and spent more than five years trying out at casting offices. "I was rejected by every casting agent in New York," said Stallone. When things were particularly tough, he even slept the night in a bus terminal, but like the character he would create, the out-of-work actor was determined not to give up.

Reaching crisis point, he sat down to write, and three-and-a-half days later, he had a script about a boxer called Rocky, who came from nowhere to a world title contest. Just as he had previously been to the casting offices, now it was a tour of the studios. Some liked the script, but were less than enthusiastic about Stallone, and made substantial offers on the proviso that he allow an established actor to play the lead role. He refused.

"Everyone wrote me off," he said, recalling his attempts to sell the script. "But it was like preparing for a fight. I always believed I would be successful. I kept hitting my head against the door, and finally, I made it." The studio capitulated. Stallone got $32,000 for the script, and a salary of almost one thousand dollars a week as an actor. He would also receive a percentage of the box office takings, and it was this that turned the hundred dollars he previously had into $10 million. Rocky won an Oscar for Best Picture, and Stallone is now one of the busiest stars in Hollywood.

From *Make Your Own Rainbow* – Leonard Ryzman

1 In what country does this story take place? Give reasons.

____

2 What do you think was the worst job Sylvester Stallone had while trying to become a star?

____

3 Because of his perseverance what had he turned his $100 into?

____

Write a short story about someone you know who has achieved what they wanted through perseverance.

Thankfulness

Introduction

THANKFULNESS – being able to express feelings of gratitude through words or actions.

- Discuss with students what is meant by the term **thankfulness**.

  Have them consider why we say thank you to other people. Are there words in other languages that express the same meaning?
- Ask students to make lists of things for which they are thankful.

My thankful list

I am thankful that I live here.
I am thankful to my parents.
I am thankful that I am a good runner.

- Students write spontaneous thank you cards to classmates, teachers, or others who have helped them in some way in the last month.
- Ask students to discuss the most appropriate ways to thank certain people. Do all people expect to be thanked? For example a teacher, dentist, doctor etc. could be said to be just doing a job they are being paid to do.

Thankfulness

Should you feel grateful when others help you? Should you expect a reward if you help another?

A group of teenagers was boarding a train for an overnight journey from London to Edinburgh. They were excited and eager and looking forward to the fun they would have.

Just as the last youth was about to board he noticed an elderly lady struggling to get into the next carriage. She was laden down by a large, cumbersome suitcase. As he made his way along the platform to assist her she suddenly fell to the ground. The youth immediately helped her up and with some effort guided her to her seat. After he had placed her bag in the luggage rack, he noticed that she was still "groggy" and uncertain after her heavy fall. He sat beside her and comforted her.

Soon, some of the teenage friends entered the carriage. "Come on Sam!" they yelled. "You're missing out on all the fun we're having."

Sam was not convinced the elderly lady was well enough to be left alone. "Don't worry about me," he said happily. "I'll come when I'm sure everything is OK."

When they left, the old lady spoke to Sam. "You go off with your friends," she said. "You're young and you can have lots of fun! I'll be alright."

"No," Sam replied. "I've got the rest of my life to have fun." Soon the pair began to chat. The old lady asked Sam about his hopes and dreams and told Sam about her life when she was young. Sam was surprised to find she had spent some time in the army and had always lived in the rainforests of the Amazon and even in Tibet. Sam was enthralled by her breathtaking stories and listened intently to every word she said.

They chatted together all through the night as the train raced northwards. They only paused occasionally to get a cup of coffee and some snacks. When they reached Edinburgh, the elderly lady thanked Sam gratefully and said how much she had enjoyed his company and appreciated what he had done for her.

"No," replied Sam, "it is me who should be grateful because your stories have enriched me greatly."

Later in life, Sam had tried many ways to make a living. None were successful and times were tough for him and his young family. One day Sam received a call from a solicitor.

"Sam, I think you should come to my office. I have some news for you," was the recorded message. A worried Sam entered the solicitor's office the next day. The solicitor looked at Sam and smiled. "I assume this will come as a shock but you have been named in a lady's will and she has left you money and property worth over a million dollars."

1. Discuss the story with your classmates.
2. If you returned money or valuables is it right to expect to be given a reward?
3. How might you thank the following people?
   - **a** your mother who sat up most of the night with you because you were sick.
   - **b** your teacher who spent all the whole of breaktime helping you with your mathematics homework.

Thankfulness

Write messages to:

a a teacher, Mr Hudson, who visited your house each week to show you how to do decimal fractions. Now you don't have any trouble with them.

b a friend, Carolyn, who visited you in hospital when you had pneumonia. She brought you some cool toys and comic books.

Dear Mr Hudson,	Dear Carolyn,
From ____________	From ____________

Values: A Programme for Primary Schools ISBN 978-184590082-3

Steadfastness

Introduction

STEADFASTNESS – being firm in purpose, faith and loyalty.

- Discuss with students what they think is meant by **steadfastness**.
- Write the word in capitals on the board. Challenge the students to make as many words as possible, in two minutes, by using the letters of steadfastness, e.g. nest, neat, east, seat, feast.
- Students research stories of the soliders who steadfastly faced death and danger to preserve our freedom. Have them share their findings.
- Being steadfast means to be able to stick to what you believe in, even when those around you are weakening. Ask students if they have ever experienced other people criticising them unfairly because of their beliefs or determination to do something. Did they give up because others criticised them?
- Have students consider the beliefs they have which will never change. What beliefs do they have now that they might change in the future?

Steadfastness

Watch Your Step

Muhammad Ali and Bev Murphy, continents apart and successful in totally different spheres of life, both told me of the same method that helped them succeed.

Muhammad Ali, former world heavyweight boxing champion, revealed how he ploughed through the difficulties of his early years. As a teenager, he experienced the grind of getting up at five every morning to do his roadwork, spending an hour on a bus to the gym for a two-hour training session, and then returning to finish house duties. Ali recalled, "I was able to continue scrubbing floors and dumping garbage by always holding in front of me my dream of becoming the world heavyweight champion."

Muhammad Ali took his career one step at a time, as did Bev Murphy, who became a training executive with the Australian Institute of Management. "To get to the top, you have to go through jobs which are often anything but glamorous, even tedious," said Bev. She started as a junior stenographer, and one of her duties was tea-making. "Each day," said Bev, "I resolved to serve the tea faster than previously, without spilling any on the saucers." This gave her a great feeling of pride.

The ancient message given by the Chinese philosopher Lao Tzu, makes good sense: "A thousand-mile journey begins with one step." Muhammad's and Bev's experiences might help us to keep that in mind.

1 In what sport did Muhammad Ali achieve greatness?

2 What helped him continue to do menial chores such as scrubbing floors?

3 To what philosophy on life does Bev Murphy credit her success?

4 Both these people were steadfast in their lives to achieve success. Can you think of any other person whose strength and resolve helped them achieve success? Describe how this happened.

5 How steadfast are you in the things you do? Would you stick up for what you believe in when others are teasing you about it?

6 Do you give up quickly when things become difficult or do you keep persevering?

7 How steadfast are you? Think about it.

Steadfastness

Have you ever set any goals for yourself? Will you be steadfast and keep these goals until you achieve them?

Share your answers with your classmates.

1 What is something you would like to achieve by the end of this term?

2 What is something you would like to achieve by the end of this year?

3 What occupation would you like to follow when you leave school?

4 What is the most important goal for you in life?

5 Do you think you will achieve this goal?

6 How might this goal change if:

a you are injured and can't walk again?

b you move to a different part of the country?

7 Is there anyone you'd like to be more friendly with?

8 What do you wish would happen?

9 What more would you like to get out of life?

10 What ambition do you have for yourself?

11 What takes too long?

12 What do you wish you had more time for?

Values: A Programme for Primary Schools ISBN 978-184590082-3

Truthfulness

Introduction

TRUTHFULNESS – being genuine and honest in all the things you say.

- Discuss with students what is meant by **truthfulness**. What are people who do not tell the truth called?
- Have students consider why people sometimes lie. Ask them to discuss the consequences of lying.
- Students role-play short stories they create about what happened when someone lied about something they had done.
- Read the story *Pinocchio* to the students. Have them illustrate the main theme of the story.

  Ask them to make up a story about a boy or girl who has hair growing on their face every time they tell a lie.
- Discuss with students the meanings of the following sayings.

The truth sometimes hurts.
Truth always wins out.

- Ask students if they have ever been tempted to tell a lie but didn't.

  Example
  - to stop being punished for something they did
  - to get something from someone

Truthfulness

Read the story and answer the questions below.

> A teacher who taught in a very tough neighbourhood was trying to impress on her class the need for honesty and truthfulness.
>
> "If you found money in the street who would keep it?" she asked.
>
> Much to her dismay all of the class raised their hand except Billy.
>
> Grateful that at least one of the class was honest she said, "Now what would you do with the money you found Billy?"
>
> "I wouldn't keep it Miss, I'd spend it!" he replied.

1 If you did something wrong and you were found out, would you ever lie to get yourself out of trouble?

____

2 *Truth is stranger than fiction*. What do you think this means?

____

____

3 Is it all right to lie at times? e.g. If a friend came to school wearing glasses for the first time you might think they look terrible but say, "They look really cool on you!" If you think there are times you can tell lies, describe one.

____

____

4 Sometimes people might tell humorous lies. *It was so wet the birds were carrying umbrellas*. Make up two of your own exaggerations.

____

____

5 Do you ever lie to make your classmates think you're cool? Role-play a story with a group in which a pupil does this and is found out.

____

____

6 Your mother is watching television and has told you that if any callers come, to tell them she is not in. There is a knock at the door and when you open it a policeman is standing there. He asks "Is your mother in?" What would you do?

____

____

Truthfulness

Have you ever thought that sometimes it may be best to tell a lie? Think carefully about these challenges. Colour **Yes** or **No** then describe why.

1 You are caught being silly when the teacher is out of the room. Is it all right to lie to get out of being punished? **YES** **NO** Why? ______________________ ______________________	**2** You saw a friend break a school window. A teacher asks who broke the window and you say, "I've got no idea." Was it right to tell the teacher this? **YES** **NO** Why? ______________________ ______________________
3 Your friend tells you his parents have split up and asks you not to tell anyone. Your mother asks you if he has said whether his parents would be at the meeting tonight. Should you tell your mother? **YES** **NO** Why? ______________________ ______________________	**4** Your teacher has given you some special homework. Nick asks you to his place after school. When you get home your mother asks if you have any homework. You say, "No." Was it right to tell your mother this? **YES** **NO** Why? ______________________ ______________________
5 You are walking home when a gang of kids threatens you. You are an only child but you tell them your big brother is not far behind. They leave. Was it right for you to tell them this? **YES** **NO** Why? ______________________ ______________________	**6** You are looking after your brother in the park. Your friends come to play. Your little brother begins to cry. One friend asks, "Is that cry baby your brother?" You say, "No." Was it right for you to say this? **YES** **NO** Why? ______________________ ______________________

Compassion

Introduction

COMPASSION – feeling sorrow or pity for others in difficulties.

- Ask students to suggest what the word **compassion** means. Encourage them to give examples.
- How can we show compassion for:
  - people who are starving
  - people who are ill
  - people who are homeless
- Students form small groups and suggest ways they can give practical help to others who are in some form of difficulty. Is there anyone in our school community who needs compassion?

No act of kindness, no matter how small, is ever wasted.
(Aesop)

- Discuss this saying with the students and have them write stories in which people display their compassion for others through kindness.
- If someone very rich gives money to an appeal for needy people just to claim it as a tax deduction, are they really compassionate? Discuss.

Compassion

A man once entered a shop and stood in front of the counter. A young assistant approached the man and asked if he could help him.
"Yes", replied the man, "I have a very large and important order I need filled." The man pulled a list from his pocket and began to read. "First of all, I need a packet of roofing nails."
"Um, yes sir," replied the young assistant and made his way to where the nails were kept. After some time searching, he found them and returned with them. "Sorry I was so long sir, but I'm new here."
"I understand," said the man gently. "Now I need a packet of 10 mm washers." He sensed the boy was flustered and nervous.
Once again the youngster took a long time to fill the order.
The manager of the store watched the boy impatiently. When the boy returned with the next items the manager rushed up, pushed the boy out of the way and said, "I'll take over Eric."
The man looked at the manager and said firmly, "I am receiving very efficient and courteous service so I would thank you to butt out!"
And with that he ignored the manager's presence and began to ask the young boy for the next item he wanted.

1 Can you explain why the man ignored the manager even though the youngster was having trouble serving him?

___

___

Now read this story

Once, a king who was victorious in battle sat on his throne as the defeated soldiers were paraded before him. One, a young boy of no more than fourteen, was thrust before him by a group of heavily-armed soldiers.
"Will we kill him Your Highness?" asked one of the triumphant soldiers.
"No," replied the king. "He is a mere youngster. Set him free to return to his native land. He can do me no harm there."
As they let him go the boy turned to the king and said, "Sire, you have shown compassion towards me. Perhaps one day I may be able to help you."
The king threw his head back and laughed loudly. "How could you ever be able to help me?"
And with that the soldiers burst into laughter also.

2 Complete this story illustrating how the boy many years later was able to help the king who had shown compassion to him.

___

___

Values: A Programme for Primary Schools ISBN 978-184590082-3

Compassion

To understand someone's problems and be able to show compassion you must first be a good listener. Write something to show that you listened and understood their problem.

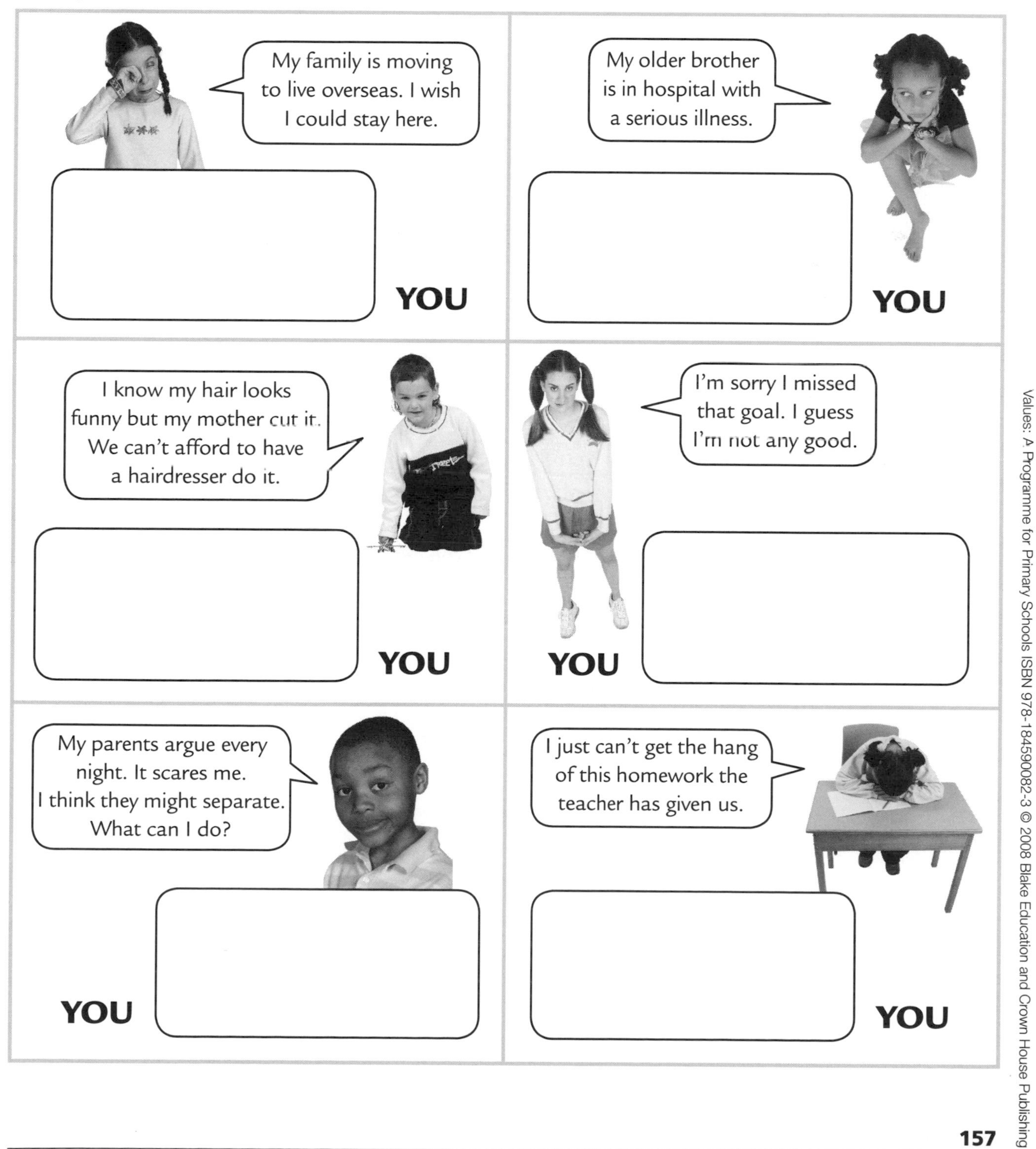

Integrity

■ Introduction

INTEGRITY – being honest and following your principles.

- Discuss with students what they think **integrity** means. Ask them to give you examples of when the word is used.
  - ◆ Live with integrity.
  - ◆ A person's integrity is measured by their conduct.
- Imagine you are a member of a special club and you promise to honour the rules of that club. Make up some rules you would expect each club member to honour. Work in small groups.

Integrity means who you are when no one is watching you.

In small groups students discuss what they think this means.

- Sometimes schools award students who show true integrity. Discuss with students the kinds of behaviour that you think should be rewarded.
- Write the following on the board.

I met a person with integrity.

Ask the students to describe what qualities they think this person will possess.

Integrity

These are some of the qualities that show integrity. For each, write a situation showing its importance.

Be honest in small things.

Be fair.

Keep your commitments.

Admit to mistakes.

Be trustworthy.

Show respect.

Values: A Programme for Primary Schoo s ISBN 978-184590082-3

Integrity 10 Chart

In the circles, write qualities that you would expect a person with integrity to possess.
Put what you think is the most important quality at the top.

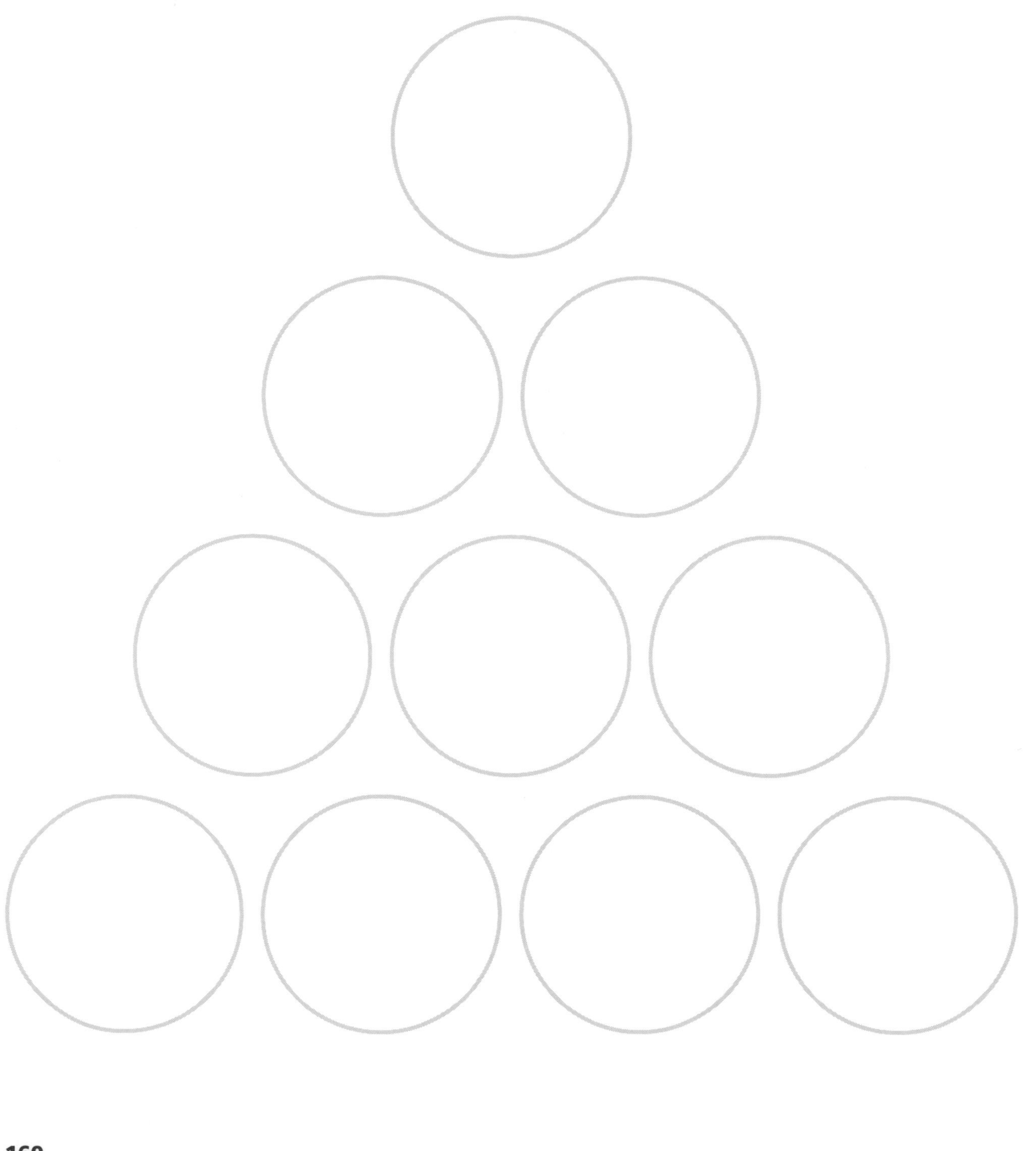

Inclusion

Introduction

INCLUSION – being included and being able to include others despite differences.

- Discuss with students what is meant by **inclusion**: the ability to accept diversity, being included in everyday activities and including others in these activities.
- Ask students to describe times they have felt bad because others have not included them in games or activities.
- Ask students to honestly tell when they have excluded others from games and activities. Why did you choose to exclude them? Do you think your decision to exclude this person was right? Was it fair?
- Have students create a colourful wall chart on **inclusion**. On the chart they list ways that they can make a newcomer feel welcome at school.

  Examples
  - I would ask her to eat with us.
  - I would ask him to play games with us.
  - We would invite her to our homes to play.
- Have the students write a class play in which one pupil plays the part of a newly-arrived pupil. Some students play the parts of those who are welcoming and tolerant while others play the roles of students who try to exclude the newcomer from class activities.
- Ask students to think of words to describe feelings that children might have when the following are heard:

  a Please come and play with us, Yuri. You'll soon learn to play rugby.

  b Clear off, Yuri. We don't want you because you don't know the rules!

Inclusion

1 Sometimes people are not included in games or activities because of their attitude and behaviour.

The students at one school listed the behaviour problems that bothered them most. Below is their list. All of the behaviours were the reasons they gave for not including some classmates in certain games.

- ☐ is too moody
- ☐ always cheats
- ☐ bullies others
- ☐ never accepts the referee's decision
- ☐ brags constantly
- ☐ talks constantly
- ☐ makes weird noises
- ☐ disrupts others playing
- ☐ has to win all the time
- ☐ abuses those who aren't as able
- ☐ tells lies
- ☐ is insulting to others

Tick the five that bother you the most. Rate these from 1 to 5 giving 1 to the behaviour you like the least.

2 Jack's parents have told him he cannot be friends with Paul, the new boy in the street. Jack likes Paul and wants to be his friend.

One day, the other boys refuse to let Paul join in the ball game they are playing in the park. Jack leaves the ball game with Paul even though he knows he will be in trouble with his parents.

The situation is:

a Jack's parents have not met Paul and have based their attitude about him on what they have heard from neighbours.

b Jack and Paul are in the same class at school and both like basketball.

Give your opinion on the story and suggest ways you might help Jack overcome his dilemma.

Inclusion

Colour red the boxes that best tell how to help newcomers feel included in everyday life. Colour grey those that would not help them.

1 teach them swear words	**2** invite them to eat lunch with your group	**3** teach them the rules of the games you play
4 explain what happens at school each day	**5** laugh and poke fun at their strange ways	**6** ask them to join your youth club
7 tell them why we like to do certain things, e.g. sports	**8** hide their pencils and books so they will get into trouble with the teachers	**9** tell them that the lollipop people at the school crossings are only there for fun and not to take any notice of them
10 teach them about things that might be dangerous, e.g. crossing a busy road	**11** invite them to talk to the whole class and describe the country they previously lived in	**12** show them how they can break school rules and get away with it
13 invite them to your home to meet your parents	**14** teach them how to steal drinks from the tuck shop	**15** tell them they must buy you sweets or else you will bash them up
16 find out what their favourite hobbies are and introduce them to others who like the same hobby	**17** show them where to catch the school bus	**18** tell them how much money you have and how good you are at all sports

Freedom

Introduction

FREEDOM – being free to make our own choices and able to accept responsibility for them.

- Read this story to the students.

  A legend tells how an old man living deep in a forest, once came across a stranger wandering past his small cottage. The stranger was carrying a wire meshed cage in which were a number of small birds.

  "What are those small birds in your cage for?" asked the old man.

  "Oh, I trap them in the forest, then sell them as cage birds at the local town market," replied the stranger.

  "Isn't that a cruel thing to do?" questioned the old man.

  "Not at all," replied the stranger. "Their owners might keep them in cages, but they get nutritious food and clean water every day. The birds want for nothing."

  "Is that so," replied the old man. "Well, in that case, I have lots of small birds in my cottage that you are welcome to have. Just follow me."

  The excited stranger immediately followed the old man to his cottage. "They are in this room," said the old man beckoning the stranger to enter.

  The stranger rushed inside expectantly. As he did so a large cage dropped over him trapping him inside its steel bars.

  "Let me out! Let me out!" yelled the frightened stranger. "I don't want to be locked in here!"

  The old man smiled mischievously. "Why not?" he asked. "I will bring you nutritious food and clean water every day. Just like the small birds you so cruelly trap. The only thing you have lost is your freedom so why are you complaining?"

  The stranger sobbed bitterly. He realised now that he had lost the most important thing in his life.

- On a sheet of paper, students make a comic strip of part of this story. Use six or more cells. Draw pictures with conversation balloons.

Freedom

Freedoms and responsibilities

Although we have certain freedoms we also have certain responsibilities, which usually accompany these freedoms. Read the statements in the boxes carefully then write whether you agree or disagree. Give your reasons.

Mike: We should have the freedom to ride our bicycles on any side of the road, on the footpath or even in the school grounds.	**Sally:** Every pupil should have the freedom to learn without the interruptions and misbehaviour of others.
Jack: Students should have the freedom to go to bed at any time they want, no matter what their age.	**Josie:** All students should have the freedom to choose their own friends, free from their parents' control.
Tegan: Students of any age should have the freedom to watch as much television as they wish.	**Paul:** All people should have the freedom to come to live in this country.

Values: A Programme for Primary Schools ISBN 978-184590082-3

Freedom

A Freedom Picture

If the number in the space is a prime number (its only factors are itself and one), colour the space.
If you do it correctly you will have a picture.

Write a paragraph explaining what the word freedom means to you.

Values: A Programme for Primary Schools ISBN 978-184590082-3

GOOD SPORTSMANSHIP

Introduction

GOOD SPORTSMANSHIP – doing all you can to win whilst showing a commitment to fair play, and concern and respect for opponents.

- Discuss with the pupils the meaning of **good sportsmanship**. They describe incidents of both good and bad sportsmanship.
- Students form small groups. Each group prepares two brief sketches – one showing good sportsmanship and one showing bad sportsmanship.
- Why is it important to show good sportsmanship?
- The following are examples of poor sportsmanship. Discuss each and on chart paper write the opposites. Head the chart **BEING A GOOD SPORT**.
  - cheating
  - losing temper
  - negative criticism of opponents
  - blaming team-mates or referees for poor play
  - showing off
  - arguing with the referees
- On the board write:

  You don't win silver, you lose gold.

  Discuss.
- Students write a paragraph explaining the statement:

  Playing fairly on and off the field is more than just winning or losing.

Good Sportsmanship

It's time to get in their face, says Warne

CHAMPION spinner Shane Warne says it's time for the Aussies to "get in the faces" of the English players in the crucial fourth Test at Trent Bridge tonight.

Australia's best player in a gripping Ashes series said relations between the two teams had been fantastic during the first three Tests, but with the series tied at one-all and the little urn up for grabs, the nice guy persona would be shelved.

"I don't think I've ever mixed with an England team like we have in this series," Warne said. "They're really good fellas and I think it comes through to everybody watching that there is a good spirit between the two teams.

"There's been great sportsmanship shown between both the teams ... (we) get along really well.

"I think both teams are enjoying the cricket that's been played."

While the cricket has been fierce, with several Australian batsmen being hit by the English fast bowlers, Warne said the Aussies had basically held their often venomous tongues.

"There hasn't been any sledging whatsoever, but that might all change at Trent Bridge," he said. "It's time to get in their faces because the Ashes are on the line. We've got to start trying to get into these blokes. I think we have probably been nice guys a bit too much so far."

Warne promised he and his teammates would crank up the intensity meter a few more notches.

"We definitely have to turn up our aggression levels and give it everything we possibly can," he said. "Our aim has to be to win this Test to go up 2-1 and retain the Ashes. I think we can do it."

Stick to the wicket, Page 106

1 What do you think Shane Warne means by "getting in the faces" of the other team players?

____

____

2 **Winning is important, but how you go about winning is the most important!** In light of this saying, do you think Shane Warne is being a good sports person?

____

____

3 When you play a game, do you abuse, name-call, cheat or even hurt your opponent so you can win?

____

4 What kind of message do you think Shane Warne is sending out to young players?

____

____

Values: A Programme for Primary Schools ISBN 978-1845900823 © 2008 Blake Education and Crown House Publishing

Good Sportsmanship

Read each of the following, then carefully consider the answer you would choose.

1 You are captain of a team playing in a netball grand final. A player on the other team is scoring lots of goals because she is tall and fast. She wears glasses. Would you:

a ask another player to stick beside her at all times?

b trip her over as she runs past?

c call her "ugly four eyes" to put her off her game?

2 Your cricket team is having difficulty getting a certain batsman out. He hits the ball in your direction and you dive to catch it. Unfortunately it hits the ground just in front of your outstretched fingers. To everyone else it looks like you have taken a wonderful catch. The referee believes it really was a catch and gives the batsman out. Would you:

a tell the referee it hit the ground first and say it wasn't out?

b leap up happily, making out it is a real catch?

c tell everyone it was a great catch?

3 Your school football team is playing against a neighbouring school. A younger boy is dominating the game. He is your opponent and he is just too fast for you. Would you:

a call him nasty names to put him off his game?

b get some team-mates to gang up on him?

c tell the captain to put another opponent on him?

4 You are playing in the under 14s international tennis championships. A girl from Uganda is beating you. She is very cool and places the ball well. Would you:

a get your friends or parents in the crowd to begin jeering her to put her off her game?

b try changing the type of game you are playing and slow down the match?

c begin yelling at the referee and disputing the calls so she will be affected?

Values definitions

Confidence — being sure of yourself.

Caring — showing concern and thoughtfulness towards others.

Kindness — being good-natured, sympathetic and kind-hearted.

Helpfulness — being unselfish and always ready to assist and share with others.

Honesty — being truthful and sincere at all times.

Courage — meeting dangers and difficulties firmly and without fear.

Respect — recognising the worth, quality and importance of others despite their differences.

Fairness — being open-minded and completely free from bias or injustice.

Loyalty — being faithful to your promises, responsibilities or undertakings.

Responsibility — being able to account for all your deeds and actions.

Values definitions *continued*

Friendliness — being kind and welcoming to others.

Pride — having a positive opinion of your own worth and being proud of your achievements.

Determination — being resolute and possessing a firmness of purpose.

Purposefulness — having the ability to achieve a desired result.

Trustworthiness — being reliable and honest at all times.

Excellence — having the ability to excel and be superior.

Doing your best — always striving to do everything to the best of your ability.

Cooperation — being able to work or act happily together with other people.

Humour — being able to perceive and express what is amusing or comical

Values definitions *continued*

Generosity – unselfish and always ready to give and to share with others.

Creativity – the ability to think and create in an original way.

Assertiveness – being prepared to take a stand on things you strongly believe in.

Patience – being calm when waiting.

Tolerance – being able to accept the differences and opinions of others without bigotry.

Forgiveness – ceasing to have bad feelings against another for what they may have done to you.

Enthusiasm – having a strong and eager interest in a particular area.

Independence – having the ability to act and work alone without the need of help from others.

Flexibility – having the ability to change or adapt to new things.

Thoughtfulness – being at all times considerate and kind to others.

Values: A Programme for Primary Schools ISBN 978-184590082-3

Values definitions *continued*

Perseverance – having the ability to continue to maintain a purpose in spite of difficulties.

Thankfulness – being able to express feelings of gratitude through words or actions.

Steadfastness – being firm in purpose, faith and loyalty.

Truthfulness – being genuine and honest in all things you say.

Compassion – feeling sorrow or pity for others in difficulties.

Integrity – being honest and following your principles.

Inclusion – being included and being able to include others despite differences.

Freedom – being free to make our own choices and able to accept responsibility for them.

Good sportsmanship – doing all you can to win whilst showing commitment to fair play and concern and respect for opponents